Windows® 8

VISUAL™

Quick Tips

Visual®

by Paul McFedries

WILEY

John Wiley & Sons, Inc.

Windows® 8 Visual™ Quick Tips

Published by
John Wiley & Sons, Inc.
10475 Crosspoint Boulevard
Indianapolis, IN 46256
www.wiley.com

Published simultaneously in Canada

Library of Congress Control Number: 2012947691

ISBN: 978-1-118-13530-3

Manufactured in the United States of America

10 9 8 7 6 5 4 3 2 1

Trademark Acknowledgments

Contact Us

For general information on our other products and services or to obtain technical support, please contact our Customer Care Department within the U.S. at 877-762-2974, outside the U.S. at 317-572-3993 or fax 317-572-4002.

For technical support please visit www.wiley.com/techsupport.

WILEY

John Wiley & Sons, Inc.

Sales

Contact Wiley at (877) 762-2974 or fax (317) 572-4002.

Credits

Executive Editor
Jody Lefevere

Sr. Project Editor
Sarah Hellert

Technical Editor
Vince Averello

Copy Editor
Marylouise Wiack

Editorial Director
Robyn Siesky

Business Manager
Amy Knies

Sr. Marketing Manager
Sandy Smith

Vice President and Executive Group Publisher
Richard Swadley

Vice President and Executive Publisher
Barry Pruett

Project Coordinator
Patrick Redmond

Graphics and Production Specialists
Ronda David-Burroughs
Jennifer Henry
Andrea Hornberger
Jill A. Proll

Quality Control Technician
Melissa Cossell

Proofreader
Sossity R. Smith

Indexer
Potomac Indexing, LLC

About the Author

Paul McFedries is a full-time technical writer. Paul has been authoring computer books since 1991 and he has more than 75 books to his credit. Paul's books have sold more than three million copies worldwide. These books include the Wiley titles *Teach Yourself VISUALLY Windows 8, Teach Yourself VISUALLY Excel 2010, The Facebook Guide for People Over 50, iPhone 4S Portable Genius,* and *The new iPad Portable Genius*. Paul is also the proprietor of Word Spy (www.wordspy.com), a website that tracks new words and phrases as they enter the language. Paul invites you to drop by his personal website at www.mcfedries.com.

Author's Acknowledgments

It goes without saying that writers focus on text, and I certainly enjoyed focusing on the text that you'll read in this book. However, this book is more than just the usual collection of words and phrases. A quick thumb through the pages will show you that this book is also chock full of images, from sharp screen shots to fun and informative illustrations. Those colorful images sure make for a beautiful book, and that beauty comes from a lot of hard work by Wiley's immensely talented group of designers and layout artists. They are all listed in the Credits section, and I thank them for creating another gem. Of course, what you read in this book must also be accurate, logically presented, and free of errors. Ensuring all of this was an excellent group of editors that included project editor Sarah Hellert, copy editor Marylouise Wiack, and technical editor Vince Averello. Thanks to all of you for your exceptional competence and hard work. Thanks, as well, to executive editor Jody Lefevere for asking me to write this book.

How to Use This Book

Who This Book Is For

This book is for readers who know the basics and want to expand their knowledge of this particular technology or software application.

The Conventions in This Book

① Steps

This book uses a step-by-step format to guide you easily through each task. Numbered steps are actions you must do; bulleted steps clarify a point, step, or optional feature; and indented steps give you the result.

② Notes

Notes give additional information — special conditions that may occur during an operation, a situation that you want to avoid, or a cross reference to a related area of the book.

③ Icons and Buttons

Icons and buttons show you exactly what you need to click to perform a step.

④ Tips

Tips offer additional information, including warnings and shortcuts.

⑤ Bold

Bold type shows text or numbers you must type.

⑥ Italics

Italic type introduces and defines a new term.

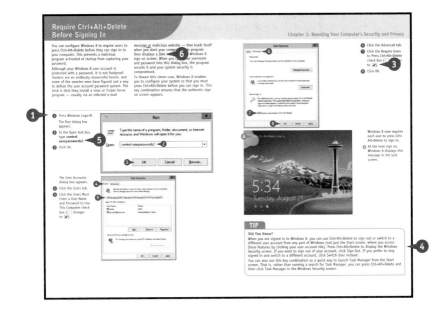

Table of Contents

Chapter 3 Boosting Your Computer's Security and Privacy

Chapter 4 Getting More Out of Files and Folders

Table of Contents

Chapter 7 Tapping Into the Power of Internet Explorer

Chapter 8 Making E-Mail Easier

Chapter 9   Enhancing Internet Security and Privacy

Chapter 10   Getting More Out of Windows 8 Networking

Optimizing the Start Screen and Taskbar

Most of what you do in Windows 8 involves the Start screen and taskbar in some way. Whether you are launching an application, starting a Windows 8 utility, adjusting settings, dealing with a notification message, or just checking the current time, you use the Start screen or taskbar to accomplish these tasks.

Because you use the Start screen and taskbar so often, it makes sense to optimize these tools to make them more efficient, which will save you time in the long run, and that is what this chapter is all about.

You begin with several techniques that make your Start screen much easier to

deal with. For example, you learn how to add new items to the Start screen, as well as how to remove items from the Start screen. You also learn how to rearrange and resize Start screen tiles. Other Start screen-related tasks include grouping apps together for easier access, adding a shutdown tile, and controlling notifications.

To help you optimize the taskbar, this chapter includes sections for pinning both programs and destinations to the taskbar, displaying clocks for other time zones, and customizing the icons in the notification area. You also learn how to access Start menu items directly from the taskbar.

Pin an Item to Your Start Screen

You can customize the Start screen to give yourself quick access to the programs that you use most often.

The items on the main Start screen — including Photos, Calendar, Mail, and Internet Explorer — are very handy because they require just one click to launch. To start up all your other programs, you must right-click the Start screen, click All Apps, and then scroll through the Apps screen to find the program you want to run. For those programs you use most often, you can avoid this extra work by *pinning* their icons permanently to the main Start screen.

All pinned program items appear to the right of the main Start screen tiles. This means that once you have pinned a program to your Start screen, you can always launch that program by scrolling right and then clicking the program icon.

① On the Start screen, begin typing the name of the program you want to pin.

② When the program appears in the Apps screen, right-click the program.

Note: *On a tablet PC, swipe down from the top edge to open the Start screen application bar, tap All Apps, and then swipe down on the program.*

Ⓐ The application bar appears.

③ Click Pin to Start.

Ⓑ Windows 8 adds a tile for the program to the Start screen.

You can remove Start screen items that you no longer use, reducing the clutter and allowing other programs that you use more often to appear.

The main part of the Start screen displays tiles for nearly twenty Windows 8 apps. This is useful because it means you can quickly and conveniently launch one of these apps with just a single mouse click or tap of the screen. However, there may be one or more apps on the main Start screen that you use only infrequently. In that case, it is best

to remove those tiles from the Start screen to make it easier to locate the rest of the Start screen apps.

Similarly, you may have pinned a program to the right of the main Start screen, as described in the previous section. By removing one or more of the default apps from the main Start screen, you bring your pinned apps to the left, making them easier to access. On the other hand, if you use a pinned program less frequently, you should remove it from the Start screen to reduce clutter.

① On the Start screen, right-click the tile of the program you want to remove.

Note: *On a tablet PC, swipe down on the tile to select it. Windows 8 indicates the selection by displaying a check mark in the upper right corner of the tile.*

Ⓐ The application bar appears.

② Click Unpin from Start.

Ⓑ Windows 8 removes the program's tile from the Start screen.

5

Rearrange Start Screen Tiles

You can customize the position and order in which the Start screen tiles appear to give yourself the quickest and most convenient access to the apps you use most often.

The default Start screen has nearly twenty tiles. It is likely that many of these tiles represent apps that you use frequently, such as Mail, Internet Explorer, People, Music, Photos, and Video. However, it is just as likely that there are apps that you only use once in a while, including Store, Maps, Weather, Camera, and SkyDrive.

Rather than removing infrequently used apps, you can instead rearrange the Start screen tiles

to make them easier to use. For example, you can move all your most-used app tiles to the left side of the Start screen. Alternatively, you might prefer to position similar apps together on the Start screen. For example, you could group together all the media apps — such as Photos, Music, and Video — or all the lifestyle apps, such as News, Sports, Travel, and Finance.

Similarly, if you have pinned some of your most-used programs to the Start screen as described earlier in this chapter, you should probably move them into the main Start screen for easier access.

---

① On the Start screen, click and drag the tile of the app you want to move.

Note: *On a tablet PC, tap and drag the app's tile.*

Ⓐ Windows 8 reduces the tile sizes slightly and adds extra space between the tiles.

② Drag the tile to the position you prefer.

③ Release the tile.

Ⓑ Windows 8 moves the tile to the new position.

You can make your Start screen more useful and efficient by resizing some of the Start screen tiles.

The Start screen supports two sizes of app tiles: small and large. They are both the same height, but the larger size is twice as wide as the smaller size. If you want to fit more tiles on your main Start screen, you can reduce the size of several tiles to create extra room. Alternatively, you might find it easier to navigate your Start screen if all or most of the tiles use the larger size.

Note that the size of the tile might determine whether you see live updating. For example, if you make the Calendar app's tile smaller, it no longer displays live updates. However, if you make the Mail app's tile smaller, it no longer shows your unread messages, but it continues to show the number of unread messages you have in your Inbox. Other apps that still show some live updates using a smaller tile are Music, Photos, Video, Weather, Store, and Finance.

Finally, note that some tiles are not resizable (this includes some Windows 8 apps and all Desktop apps), so the technique in this section will not work for some tiles.

1 Right-click the Start screen tile you want to resize.

A Windows 8 displays the application bar.

2 Click Smaller.

Note: *If the tile is small and you prefer to enlarge it, click Larger instead.*

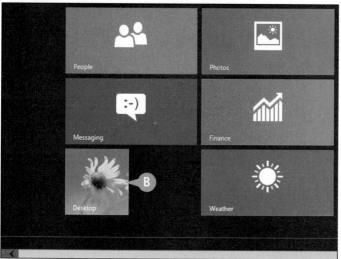

B Windows 8 resizes the tile.

Show the Administrative Tools on the Start Screen

You can give yourself easy access to some useful and powerful Windows 8 features by adding the administrative tools to the Start screen.

Windows 8 ships with a collection of advanced features called the administrative tools. These tools include Performance Monitor for tracking performance on your PC; Task Scheduler for scheduling programs and scripts; Disk Cleanup for deleting unnecessary files; Computer Management for performing tasks such as dealing with devices, configuring disk drives, and working with users; and Defragment and Optimize Drives for defragmenting your hard drive.

Some administrative tools are relatively easy to run. For example, press Windows Logo+X to display a menu that includes Event Viewer, Disk Management, and a few other administrative tools. However, the rest of these tools are difficult to access in Windows 8. For example, to run the Task Scheduler, press Windows Logo+W, type **task**, and then click Schedule tasks. Other administrative tools require you to know the program filename. For example, to run the System Configuration utility, press Windows Logo+R, type **msconfig**, and then click OK.

If you find that you use one or more of these tools frequently, or if you do not know how to launch any of these tools, you can save time by displaying the administrative tools as tiles on the Start screen.

① Move the mouse pointer to the upper right corner of the screen.

Ⓐ Windows 8 displays the Charms menu.

Note: *You can also display the Charms menu by pressing Windows Logo+C.*

② Click Settings.

The Settings pane appears.

Note: *You can also access the Settings pane directly by pressing Windows Logo+I.*

③ Click Tiles.

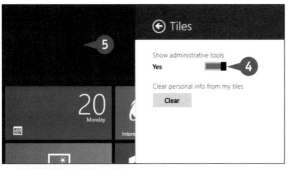

The Start settings pane appears.

④ Click the Show Administrative Tools switch to Yes.

⑤ Click the Start screen.

Ⓑ The administrative tools appear as tiles on the Start screen.

Did You Know?

Here is a summary of what you can do with the administrative tools:

Computer Management — Manage your Windows 8 computer.

Component Services — Display the Component Services window.

Defragment and Optimize Drives — Defragment your hard drive.

Disk Cleanup — Delete unnecessary files.

Event Viewer — Examine the Windows 8 list of events.

iSCSI Initiator — Manage connections to iSCSI devices.

Local Security Policy — Set up security policies on your system.

ODBC Data Sources — Create and work with data sources.

Performance Monitor — Monitor the performance of your system.

Print Management — Manage, share, and deploy printers and print servers.

Resource Monitor — View the resources being used by your PC.

Services — Control the system services.

System Configuration — Configure your PC.

System Information — View data about your PC.

Task Scheduler — Run programs or scripts on a schedule.

Windows Firewall with Advanced Security — Control the Windows 8 firewall.

Windows Memory Diagnostic — Check your computer's memory chips for problems.

Windows PowerShell ISE — Create PowerShell scripts.

Create an App Group

You can make your Start screen much more efficient and easier to use by organizing some or all of your tiles into groups of related apps.

In Windows 8, the default arrangement of Start screen tiles includes two app groups that are separated by a relatively wide vertical strip of empty Start screen space.

These default groups are not particularly useful because they do not contain related apps. It might be better to have, say, all the media apps (such as Music, Photos, Video, and Camera) in one group, and all the communications apps (such as Mail, People, Messaging, and Calendar)

in another. You can certainly use the technique for rearranging Start screen tiles, shown earlier in this chapter, to improve these default groups.

However, Windows 8 also enables you to create your own groups. For example, you might want to break out all the game-related apps into their own group. Similarly, if you added the administrative tools to the Start screen as described in the previous section, you might want to place those app tiles in their own group. Even better, Windows 8 also enables you to add names to each group, which makes them even easier to use and navigate.

Add App Tiles to a New Group

1. Drag the first app tile all the way to the left edge of the screen.

A. Windows 8 displays a vertical bar.

2. Release the mouse button to drop the app tile.

B. Windows 8 creates a new group for the app tile.

3. To add other tiles to the new group, drag and drop the tiles within the group.

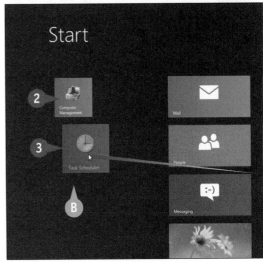

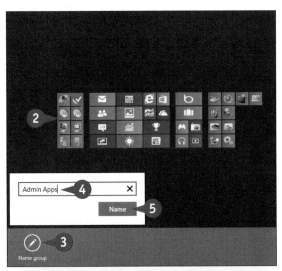

Name the New Group

1 Press Ctrl+- (dash) to zoom out of the Start screen.

2 Right-click any tile in the group.

3 Click Name Group.

Windows 8 prompts you to enter a group name.

4 Type the group name.

5 Click Name.

Windows 8 applies the name to the group.

6 Press Ctrl++ (plus) to zoom back in to the Start screen.

C Windows 8 displays the name above the group.

TIPS

More Options!
You can rearrange your groups within the Start screen to make some groups more accessible by moving them closer to the left side of the Start screen. To move a group, press Ctrl+- to zoom out of the Start screen. Use your mouse (or your finger or a stylus on a tablet) to drag the group you want to move and then drop it in the position you prefer.

Try This!
You can quickly add a tile to a group. On the Start screen, use your mouse (or your finger or a stylus if you have a tablet PC) to drag the app tile down toward the bottom edge of the screen. When the app tile hits the bottom edge, Windows 8 automatically zooms out. Drag the tile into the group (at this point, Windows 8 automatically zooms back in to the Start screen) and then drop the tile within the group.

Add a Shutdown Tile to the Start Screen

You can make it much more convenient to shut down your computer by adding a tile to the Start screen that performs the shutdown task.

The new Start screen is useful for accessing Windows 8 apps, but it makes many other Windows tasks unnecessarily difficult or inefficient. Shutting down your computer is one of those tasks that is much less efficient in Windows 8.

For example, to shut down your computer using the mouse, you must move the pointer to the upper right corner of the screen to display the

Charms menu, click Settings to open the Start settings pane, click Power, and then click Shutdown. You can speed things up by pressing Windows Logo+I to go directly to the Start settings pane, but then you have to switch back to the mouse to continue.

A much better solution is to create a new Start screen tile that runs the shutdown command. That way, you can shut down your computer with just the click of a mouse.

Create a Shutdown Shortcut

1 Click the Desktop tile.

Windows 8 displays the desktop.

Note: *You can also switch to the desktop by pressing Windows Logo+D.*

2 Right-click the desktop.

3 Click New.

4 Click Shortcut.

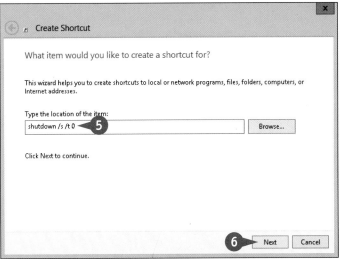

The Create Shortcut dialog box appears.

⑤ Type **shutdown /s /t 0**.

Note: *The last character in the command above is the number zero.*

⑥ Click Next.

Windows 8 prompts you to name the shortcut.

⑦ Type the name you want to use.

Note: *The name you type is the name that will appear on the Start screen.*

⑧ Click Finish.

TIP

More Options!
You might find that you restart your computer more than you shut it down. In that case, consider creating a restart shortcut, instead. To do that, in step 5 when you enter the command that you want the shortcut to run, type **shutdown /r /t 0**.
As before, the last character in the command is the number zero.

continued ►

You can make your shutdown tile easier to locate as well as add visual interest to the Start screen by customizing the icon used by the shortcut file.

When you create a shortcut, Windows 8 applies a generic icon to the file. Certainly if you plan on adding multiple shortcuts to the Start screen (for example, you might want to also add a restart shortcut), using the generic icon for each tile can be confusing. Not only that, but the default shortcut icon is not very pleasing to the eye.

To help you differentiate your shortcut tiles, and to add some eye candy to the Start screen, you can select a different icon for your shortcut file.

Change the Shortcut Icon

① Right-click the shutdown shortcut.

② Click Properties.

The shortcut's Properties dialog box appears.

③ Click Change Icon.

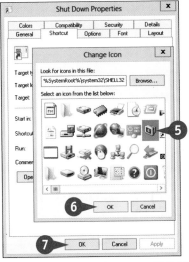

Windows 8 warns you that the shutdown command contains no icons.

④ Click OK.

The Change Icon dialog box appears.

⑤ Click the icon you want to use.

⑥ Click OK.

⑦ Click OK.

Pin the Shortcut to the Start Screen

① Right-click the shortcut.

② Click Pin to Start.

Windows 8 adds the shortcut to the Start screen.

Control App Notifications

You can gain control over the way that Windows 8 displays app notifications as well as turn off notifications for individual apps.

Windows 8 keeps you in the loop by displaying notifications whenever certain applications have messages that they want you to see. For example, if you receive a new instant message, the Messaging app plays a sound and displays the message and the person who sent it in a notification that appears in the upper right corner of the Start screen or any Windows 8 app you are using, or in the lock screen.

This is handy behavior, but you might prefer to turn off app notifications for a while if you do not want to be disturbed. Similarly, if there is a particular app that you do not want to hear from, you can turn off individual app notifications.

① Press Windows Logo+I.

The Settings pane appears.

② Click Change PC Settings.

The PC Settings screen appears.

③ Click Notifications.

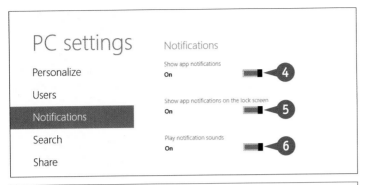

The Notifications settings appear.

④ If you do not want to see any notifications, click Show App Notifications to Off.

⑤ If you do not want to see any notifications in the lock screen, click Show App Notifications On the Lock Screen to Off.

⑥ If you do not want to hear the notification sound, click Play Notification Sounds to Off.

⑦ In the Show Notifications from These Apps section, for each app from which you no longer want to see notifications, click the switch to Off.

Restore the Start Menu to the Taskbar

If you find that you do most of your work in the Windows 8 desktop rather than the Start screen, you can make your life easier and more efficient by adding the Start menu to the taskbar.

The Start screen and Windows 8 apps are an interesting departure for Microsoft, but they are not to everyone's taste. Therefore, you might find yourself spending the bulk of your Windows 8 time using the desktop. Rather than constantly switching back to the Start screen to launch Desktop apps, you can add the Start menu directly to the taskbar.

Note, however, that this is not the old Start menu from previous versions of Windows. Instead, it is just the Start Menu folder added to the taskbar as a toolbar. Still, it does give you access to many desktop tools, including system tools, accessories, and the administrative tools.

① On the Start screen, click the Desktop tile.

Note: *You can also display the desktop by pressing Windows Logo+D.*

The Windows 8 desktop appears.

② Right-click an empty section of the taskbar.

③ Click Toolbars.

④ Click New Toolbar.

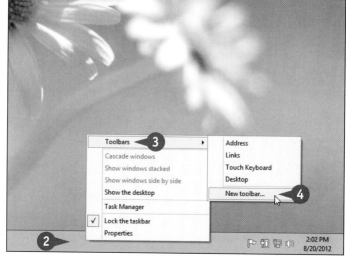

The New Toolbar - Choose a Folder dialog box appears.

⑤ Click an empty section of the address bar and then type the following folder path:

C:\ProgramData\ Microsoft\Windows\ Start Menu.

⑥ Press Enter.

⑦ Click Select Folder.

Ⓐ Windows 8 adds the Start Menu folder as a taskbar toolbar.

⑧ Click the toolbar arrows.

Ⓑ Use the subfolders to launch Start menu programs and tools.

TIP

Remove It!

You might decide that you do not want to clutter the taskbar with the Start Menu toolbar. For example, if you pin many programs to the taskbar as described in the next section, you might want some extra room for another pinned program.

To remove the Start Menu toolbar, right-click the taskbar, click Toolbars, and then click the Start Menu toolbar.

Pin a Program to the Taskbar

If you find yourself spending time in the Windows 8 desktop more often than the Start screen, you can place your favorite programs a mouse click away by pinning them to the Windows 8 taskbar.

In this chapter's first section, you learned how to pin a program icon to the Start screen. However, that is only useful if you use the Start screen regularly. If you use the desktop most of the time and you have a program that you use frequently, you might prefer to have that program just a single click away. You can

achieve this by pinning that program to the Windows 8 taskbar.

As with previous versions of Windows, the Windows 8 taskbar displays an icon for each running program. However, you can also use the taskbar to store program icons. Once you have a shortcut icon for a program pinned to the taskbar, you can then launch that program just by clicking the icon.

You can pin a program to the taskbar either from the Start screen or from the desktop.

Pin a Program Using the Start Screen

1. On the Start screen, type the name of the program you want to pin.

2. In the Apps screen search results, right-click the program you want to pin.

3. Click Pin to Taskbar.

   Windows 8 adds an icon for the program to the taskbar.

Pin a Running Program

1. Launch the program you want to pin.

2. Right-click the running program's taskbar icon.

3. Click Pin This Program to Taskbar.

   Windows 8 adds an icon for the program to the taskbar.

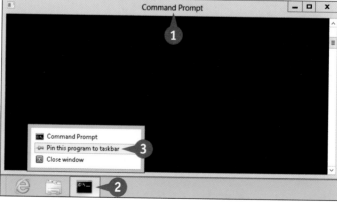

Pin a Program Using the Start Menu

1 Add the Start Menu toolbar to the taskbar as described in the previous section.

2 Click the Start Menu toolbar arrows.

3 If necessary, open the submenu that contains the program you want to pin to the taskbar. For example, if the program is in the Accessories submenu, click Programs and then click Windows Accessories.

4 Click and drag the program icon to any empty section of the taskbar.

5 When you see the Pin to Taskbar banner, drop the icon.

Windows 8 adds an icon for the program to the taskbar.

TIPS

Taskbar Trick!
As you drop program icons onto the taskbar, Windows 8 displays the icons left to right in the order you added them. If you prefer a different order, click and drag a taskbar icon to the left or right and then drop it in the new position. Note that this technique applies not only to the icons pinned to the taskbar, but also to the icons for any running programs.

Remove It!
If you decide you no longer require a program to be pinned to the taskbar, you should remove it to reduce taskbar clutter and provide more room for other taskbar icons. To remove a pinned program icon, right-click the icon and then click Unpin this Program from Taskbar.

21

Pin a Destination to a Taskbar Icon

If you often use the Windows 8 desktop, you can pin a destination such as a folder, document, or website to a taskbar icon for easy access.

In the previous section, "Pin a Program to the Taskbar," you learned how to add icons for your favorite programs to the taskbar so that you could launch any of those programs with a single click. However, rather than favorite programs, you might have favorite folders, documents, music tracks, or websites that you launch frequently. Windows 8 calls these items *destinations*.

Although you cannot pin destinations directly to the taskbar, you can pin them to the jump list associated with a taskbar icon. This means that you can launch a destination by right-clicking its program's taskbar icon and then clicking the destination in the jump list. This is generally much quicker than running the program and opening the destination using the program's commands.

You can pin a destination to a taskbar icon either by running the Pin to this List command, or by clicking and dragging a destination to the taskbar icon.

Pin a Destination Using a Command

① Right-click the taskbar icon of the program associated with the destination.

② Move the mouse pointer over the destination icon.

Note: *If you do not see the destination in the jump list, you must use the mouse method described in the next set of steps.*

③ Click Pin to this List.

Ⓐ You can also click the Pin to this List icon.

Ⓑ Windows 8 adds an icon for the destination to the Pinned section of the program's jump list.

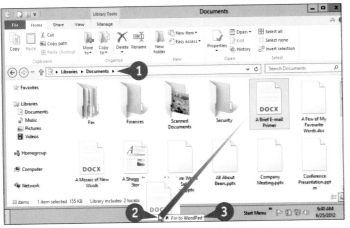

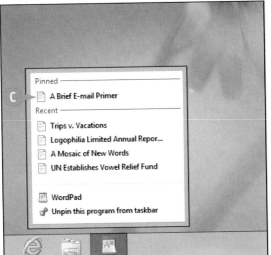

Pin a Destination Using Your Mouse

1 Open the folder that contains the item you want to pin.

2 Click and drag the icon to any empty section of the taskbar.

3 When you see the Pin to *Program* banner (where *Program* is the name of the application associated with the destination), drop the icon.

C Windows 8 adds an icon for the destination to the Pinned section of the program's jump list.

TIPS

Taskbar Trick!

If the program associated with the destination does not already have a taskbar icon, you do not need to pin the program to the taskbar separately. Instead, follow steps 1 to 3 in the second set of steps to drop the destination on an empty section of the taskbar. Windows 8 adds a new icon for the program to the taskbar and pins the destination to the program's jump list.

Remove It!

If you no longer require a destination to be pinned to its program's taskbar icon, you can remove it to reduce clutter in the jump list and provide more room for other destinations. To remove a pinned destination, right-click the icon and then click Unpin from this List. You can also click the Unpin from this List icon (☑) that appears to the right of the destination.

Display a Clock for Another Time Zone

If you deal with people in another time zone, you can make it easier to find out the current time in that zone by customizing the Windows 8 desktop to show a second clock configured for the time zone.

If you have colleagues, friends, or family members who work or live in a different time zone, it is often important to know the correct time in that zone. For example, you would not want to call someone at home at 9 a.m. your time if that person lives in a time zone three

hours behind you. Similarly, if you know that a business colleague leaves work at 5 p.m. and that person works in a time zone seven hours ahead of you, then you know that any calls you place to that person must occur before 10 a.m. your time.

If you need to be sure about the current time in another time zone, you can customize the Windows 8 date and time display to show not only your current time, but also the current time in the other time zone.

---

① Press Windows Logo+D to display the Windows 8 desktop.

② Click the time.

③ Click Change Date and Time Settings.

The Date and Time dialog box appears.

④ Click the Additional Clocks tab.

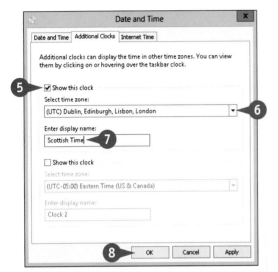

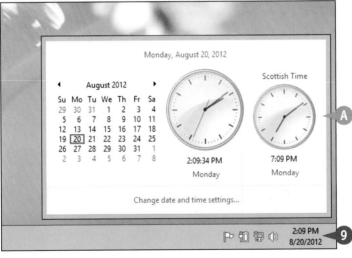

⑤ Click the Show this Clock check box (☐ changes to ✔).

⑥ Click here and then click the time zone you want to use in the new clock.

⑦ Type a name for the new clock.

⑧ Click OK.

Windows 8 adds the clock.

⑨ Click the time.

Ⓐ Windows 8 displays the extra clock.

Note: If you position the mouse pointer over the time, Windows 8 displays a banner that shows the current date, your current local time, and the current time in the other time zone.

TIPS

Did You Know?

After you customize Windows 8 with the extra clock, you normally click the time in the notification area to see both clocks. However, if you just position the mouse pointer over the time, Windows 8 displays a banner that shows the current date, your current local time, and the current time in the other time zone.

More Options!

If you deal with people in a third time zone, you can customize Windows 8 to display a third clock. Follow steps 1 to 4 to display the Additional Clocks tab. Click the second Show this Clock check box (☐ changes to ✔), click the down arrow in the list below it to select a time zone, type a name for the third clock, and then click OK.

Control Taskbar Notifications

When you are using the Windows 8 desktop, you can customize the way that Windows 8 displays the icons in the notification area to ensure a particular icon is always visible or to turn off an icon's notifications.

The notification area in the Windows 8 taskbar shows only a few icons: Volume, Network, and Action Center, and notebook PCs also show the Power icon. All other Windows 8 icons and third-party program icons are hidden, and you access them by clicking the Show Hidden Icons arrow to

the left of the notification area. However, Windows 8 does display all notifications generated by the hidden icons, so you never miss important messages.

In certain cases you might want to customize the default arrangement. For example, many notification icons offer quick access to their programs' features when you right-click them. If there is an icon that you right-click frequently, you might want to configure the notification area to show the icon on the taskbar.

1 Press Windows Logo+D to display the Windows 8 desktop.

2 Click the Show Hidden Icons arrow.

3 Click Customize.

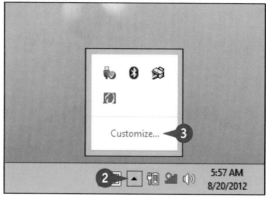

The Notification Area Icons window appears.

4 Click here and then click an option:

Show Icon and Notifications: Displays the icon on the taskbar and shows its notifications.

Hide Icon and Notifications: Does not display the icon or its notifications.

Only Show Notifications: Hides the icon, but displays its notifications.

5 Repeat step 4 for the other icons you want to configure.

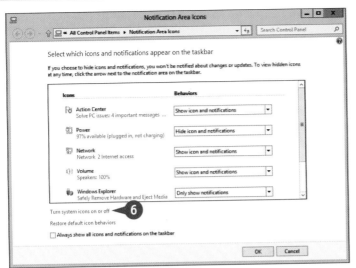

6 Click Turn System Icons On or Off.

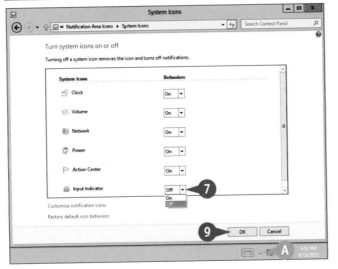

7 Click here and then click Off to prevent a system icon from appearing in the notification area.

8 Repeat step 7 for each system icon you want to hide.

9 Click OK to return to the Notification Area Icons window.

10 Click OK (not shown).

Windows 8 puts the new settings into effect.

A Click this arrow to see your hidden icons.

TIP

Did You Know?

You can configure the notification area to always show all the icons and their notifications. Follow steps 1 to 3 to open the Notification Area Icons window. Click the Always Show All Icons and Notifications on the Taskbar check box (☐ changes to ☑), and then click OK.

Chapter 2

Configuring Windows 8 to Suit the Way You Work

Windows 8 is endlessly customizable and offers many features that enable you to modify the look and feel of your system to suit your style and the way you work.

You probably already know how to customize aspects of the Windows 8 screen, such as the colors, fonts, desktop background, and screen resolution. These are useful techniques to know, to be sure, but Windows 8 offers a number of other techniques that put much more emphasis on what is practical. That is, although changing your screen colors might make Windows 8 more interesting, it does not help you get your work done

any faster. However, techniques such as logging on automatically, customizing app searches, showing more apps in the lock screen, and synchronizing your settings between two or more devices can help you work faster and better.

This chapter focuses not only on aspects of customizing Windows 8 that are designed to save you time, but also those that help you get more out of your Windows 8 system. For example, in this chapter you learn how to add a second monitor, add another administrator account, and customize the Explorer Quick Access Toolbar.

Change Your User Account Picture

You can customize your Windows 8 user account to use a picture that suits you.

When you install Windows 8, the program takes you through several tasks, including choosing a username and password. However, it does not ask you to select a picture to go along with your user account. Instead, Windows 8 just supplies your account with a generic illustration, or whatever image your Microsoft Live account uses. This picture appears in the top right corner of the Start screen, the logon screen, and the Users section of the PC Settings screen. So

rather than using the default illustration, you might prefer to use a photo or other artwork.

In that case, you can configure your user account to use another picture. If your computer already contains the image you want to use, you choose your own image. You can use any picture you want, as long as it is in one of the four image file types that Windows 8 supports: Bitmap, JPEG, GIF, or PNG. Alternatively, you can also use your computer's webcam to take your picture.

---

1 Press Windows Logo+W.

The Settings search pane appears.

2 Type **picture**.

3 Click Account Picture.

The PC Settings app appears, showing the Personalize tab with the Account Picture subtab selected.

4 Click Browse.

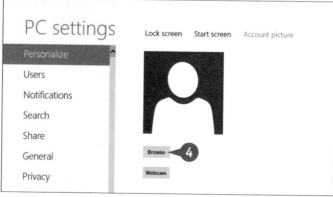

The Account Pictures folder appears.

5 Choose the folder that contains the image you want to use.

6 Click the image.

7 Click Choose Image.

A Windows 8 applies the new picture to your user account.

TIP

More Options!

If your computer comes with a webcam or you have a similar camera attached to your PC, you can use the camera to take your account picture. Follow steps 1 to 3 to open the Account Picture tab and then click Camera to open the Camera app. Compose your shot and then click the screen to take the picture. Click and drag the account picture box to set the image area, and then click OK.

If you prefer to use a short (up to five seconds) video instead, then click the Video Mode button to switch to video mode, click the screen to begin recording, and then click the screen again when the recording is complete. Click OK to set the video as your account picture.

Disable the Lock Screen

You can make it easier to log on to Windows 8 and to unlock your PC by disabling the Windows 8 lock screen.

The Windows 8 lock screen appears when you start your PC and when you lock your PC. The lock screen shows the current date and time, and also includes icons that tell you information about certain apps, such as how many unread e-mail messages you have.

The lock screen can be useful, but it also slows you down because it must be dismissed before your can log on or unlock your PC. You do this by pressing Enter or by dragging the lock screen up to reveal the logon screen.

To avoid this extra step, you can configure Windows 8 to disable the lock screen. This means you do not see the lock screen when you log on or when you lock your computer. Instead, Windows 8 takes you directly to the logon screen.

---

1 On the Start screen, type **gpedit.msc**.

Windows 8 displays the Apps search results.

2 Click gpedit in the search results.

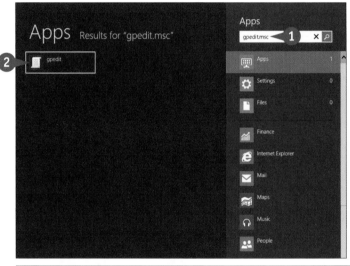

The Local Group Policy Editor appears.

3 Under Computer Configuration, open the Administrative Templates branch.

4 Open the Control Panel branch.

5 Click Personalization.

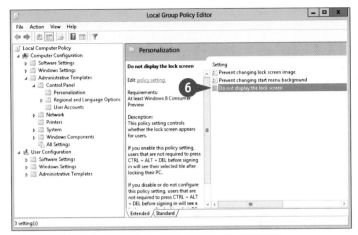

The Personalization policies appear.

⑥ Double-click the Do Not Display the Lock Screen policy.

The policy details appear.

⑦ Click Enabled (○ changes to ◉).

⑧ Click OK.

Windows 8 puts the new policy into effect.

TIP

Important!
In Chapter 3, you learn how to configure your PC to require that users press Ctrl+Alt+Delete before they log on. This is a useful security measure, but if you implement it, then Windows 8 ignores the Do Not Display the Lock Screen policy setting. This makes sense because disabling the lock screen would eliminate the security benefit of requiring Ctrl+Alt+Delete.

Configure Windows 8 to Work with a Second Monitor

You can improve your productivity and efficiency by configuring Windows 8 to extend the Start screen and desktop across two monitors.

Over the past few years, many studies have shown that you can greatly improve your productivity by doing one thing: adding a second monitor to your system. This enables you to have whatever program you are currently working with displayed on one monitor, and your reference materials, e-mail program, or some other secondary program on the second monitor. This is more efficient because you no longer have to switch back and forth between the two programs.

To work with two monitors on a single computer, one solution is to install a second video card and attach the second monitor to it. However, many video cards now come with dual output ports: either one VGA port and one DVI port, or two DVI ports. Choose a card that matches the ports on your monitors.

Once you have installed the new video card and attached the monitors, you then need to configure Windows 8 to extend the Start screen and desktop across both monitors and choose which monitor is the main display that shows the Start screen and taskbar.

Extend to a Second Screen

1. Connect the second monitor to your Windows PC.

2. Press Windows Logo+K.

   Windows 8 displays the Devices pane.

3. Click Second Screen.

The Second Screen pane appears.

Note: You can jump directly to the Second Screen pane by pressing Windows Logo+P.

4. Click Extend.

   Windows 8 connects to the second monitor and uses it to display the Desktop app.

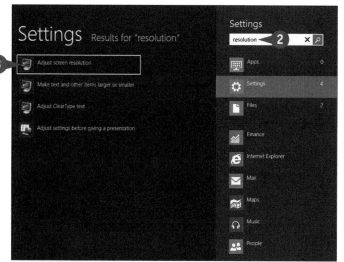

Set the Main Display

① Press Windows Logo+W.

The Settings search pane appears.

② Type **resolution**.

③ Click Adjust Screen Resolution.

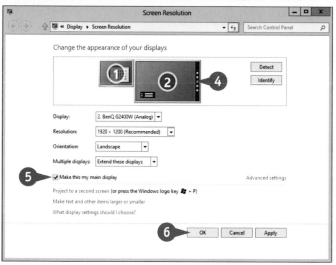

The Screen Resolution dialog box appears on the desktop.

④ Click the monitor you want to set as the main monitor.

⑤ Click the Make This My Main Display check box (☐ changes to ☑).

⑥ Click OK.

TIPS

More Options!

Ideally, you should be able to move your mouse continuously from the left monitor to the right monitor. If you find that the mouse stops at the right edge of your left monitor, it means you need to exchange the icons of the left and right monitors. To do that, click and drag the left monitor icon to the right of the other monitor icon (or vice versa).

Remove It!

If you need to use the second monitor elsewhere, you should remove it from Windows 8 and revert to using a single screen. To do this, press Windows Logo+P to open the Second Screen pane, and then click PC Screen Only.

35

Remove Apps from Search

You can make it easier to run a search on various apps by removing any apps you never use for searching.

Windows 8 introduces a new search system that enables you to search for a particular term across multiple apps. For example, if you are currently using the Internet Explorer app and you bring up the Search pane, you could use it to run a search for Indianapolis using the Bing search engine. Without leaving the Search pane, you could also click Maps to search for Indianapolis in the Maps

app; click Weather to see the current weather in Indianapolis using the Weather app; or click Mail to search for messages that include the word "Indianapolis."

This makes it easy to search just the apps you want. To make it even easier, you can remove any apps that you never use for searching. For example, if you never search the Finance app, you can remove it from the Search pane to make it easier to find and select the rest of the apps.

① Press Windows Logo+I.

Windows 8 displays the Settings pane.

Note: *On a tablet, swipe in from the right edge and then tap Settings.*

② Click Change PC Settings.

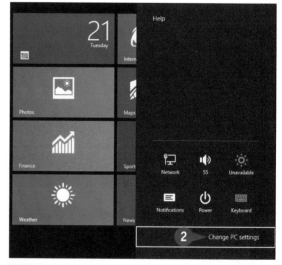

Windows 8 opens the PC Settings screen.

③ Click Search.

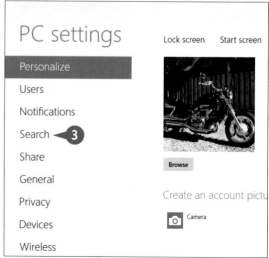

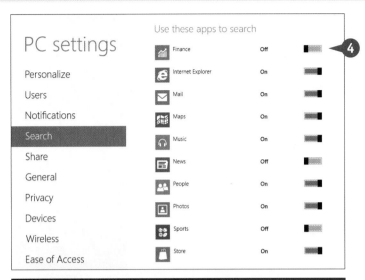

④ Click the switch to Off beside each app you want to exclude from the Search pane.

⑤ Press Windows Logo to return to the Start screen.

⑥ Press Windows Logo+Q.

Windows 8 opens the Search pane.

Ⓐ The apps you excluded in step 4 do not appear in the Search pane.

TIP

More Options!

When you first open the Search pane, the apps appear in alphabetical order. By default, Windows 8 keeps track of which apps you use to search. After you have used the Search pane for a while, Windows 8 begins sorting the apps to show the ones you use most often at the top. This usually makes it easier to find your most-searched apps.

However, if the apps change positions frequently, you might find this makes it harder to locate the one you want. If so, you can turn off the sorting feature. Press Windows Logo+I, click Change PC Settings, click Search, and then click the Show the Apps I Search Most Often at the Top switch to Off.

37

Turn Off Notifications for an App

You can avoid being unnecessarily distracted by a particular app by turning off notifications for that app.

An app notification is a message that appears in the upper right corner of the screen when an application has information to impart. This could be a new text message or e-mail, or a message letting you know some operation has completed.

App notifications can be useful if you want to know what is going on in another app without having to switch to that app. However, app notifications can also distract you from your current work by focusing your attention elsewhere. That is, not only do you take your eye off your current task to view the notification, but the notification message itself might cause you to begin thinking about the content of the message.

If you find that a certain app is particularly distracting (either in its frequency or its content), then you can tell Windows 8 to no longer display notifications for that app.

---

① Move the mouse pointer to the top right corner of the screen.

Windows 8 displays the Charms menu.

Note: *You can also press Windows Logo+C. On a tablet, swipe in from the right edge to display the Charms menu.*

② Click Settings.

Windows 8 displays the Settings pane.

Note: *You can also display the Settings pane by pressing Windows Logo+I.*

③ Click Change PC Settings.

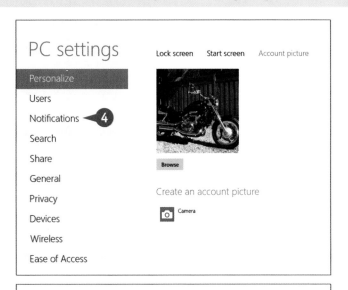

Windows 8 opens the PC Settings screen.

④ Click Notifications.

Windows 8 displays the Notifications settings.

⑤ Click the switch to Off beside each app you want to prevent from displaying notifications.

TIPS

More Options!
Although handy, app notifications tend to distract you from whatever you are currently working on. That might be what you want if you are waiting for something important, but you might find it overly distracting at other times. In that case, you can disable all app notifications to avoid being disturbed while you work. Follow steps 1 to 4 to open the Notifications settings, and then click the Show App Notifications switch to Off.

More Options!
Many people find that the most distracting thing about app notifications is not the notifications themselves, but the sound that Windows 8 plays as it displays them. To shut off this sound, follow steps 1 to 4 to open the Notifications settings, and then click the Play Notification Sounds switch to Off.

Add an App to the Lock Screen

If you frequently lock your computer, you can make the resulting lock screen more useful by adding one or more apps to the lock screen.

As you learn in Chapter 3, locking your computer is a useful safety feature because it prevents unauthorized users from accessing your files and your network. When you lock your PC, Windows 8 displays the lock screen, which includes the current date and time, an icon that shows the current network status, and an icon that shows the current power state of your computer (that

is, either plugged in or on battery). By default, Windows 8 also includes icons for apps that have had recent notifications. For example, the Mail app shows the number of unread messages and the Messaging app shows the number of new text messages. The lock screen also shows any new notifications that appear for these apps.

If you lock your computer frequently, you can make the lock screen even more useful by adding icons for other apps that support notifications.

---

1 Press Windows Logo+I.

Windows 8 displays the Settings pane.

Note: *On a tablet, swipe in from the right edge and then tap Settings.*

2 Click Change PC Settings.

Windows 8 opens the PC Settings screen.

3 Click Personalize.

4 Click the Lock Screen tab.

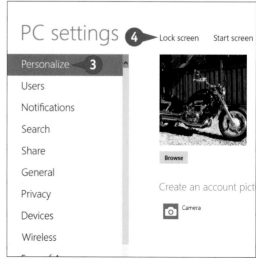

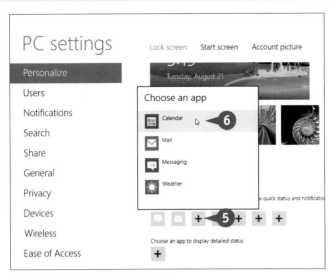

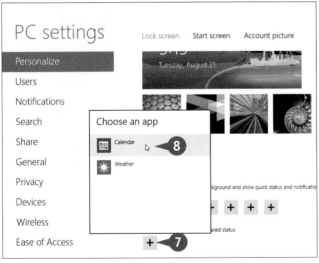

⑤ Click +.

Windows 8 opens the Choose an App window.

⑥ Click the app you want to add to the lock screen.

⑦ To select an app to display its detailed status, click +.

⑧ Click the app.

Windows 8 puts the new settings into effect and the apps appear in the lock screen the next time you use it.

TIP

Customize It!

If you use the lock screen frequently, you might prefer to view a background image that is different from the default image. To choose a different lock screen background, follow steps 1 to 4 to display the Lock Screen tab, and then click one of the default images.

Alternatively, you can choose your own image by clicking Browse, opening the folder that contains the image you want to use, clicking the image, and then clicking Choose Picture.

Add Another Administrator Account

You can make Windows 8 easier and more efficient for another user by enabling or creating an administrator-level account for that user.

When you create your first account during the initial Windows 8 configuration routine, that account is set up as an administrative account (technically, it is added to the Administrators security group). Administrative accounts are very powerful because they perform tasks such as creating new user accounts, adjusting system settings, and installing programs.

Each subsequent account you create in Windows 8 is a standard user account (technically, it is a member of the Users security group), and so it is limited in what it can do. These user accounts are fine for performing day-to-day tasks in Windows 8, but there are many Windows 8 tasks that are off-limits to these accounts.

If you have a user who feels restricted by the limitations of a standard user account, and who you feel is trustworthy enough to handle more responsibility, you can give that person an administrative-level account. You can do this either by enabling the existing administrator account or by creating a new account and adding it to the Administrators group.

Enable the Existing Administrator Account

1. On the Start screen, type **lusrmgr.msc**.

2. Click lusrmgr icon in the search results.

The Local Users and Groups window appears.

3. Click Users.

4. Double-click Administrator.

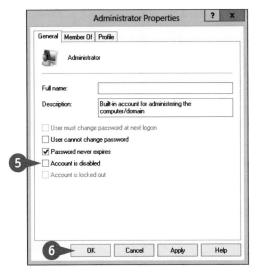

The Administrator Properties dialog box appears.

5 Click Account is Disabled ($\checkmark$ changes to $\square$).

6 Click OK.

Windows 8 enables the administrator account.

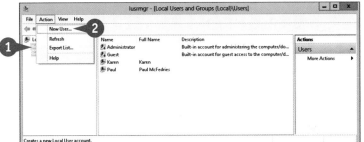

Create a New Administrator Account

1 Follow steps 1 to 3 in the previous set of steps to open the Local Users and Groups window and select the Users folder.

2 Click Action and then click New User.

TIPS

Secure It!
The built-in administrator account does *not* come with a password. This is a very dangerous situation, so you should assign a password to this account immediately. In the Local Users and Groups window, right-click the administrator account, click Set Password, and then click Proceed when Windows 8 asks you to confirm. Type the new password (twice) and then click OK.

Change It!
The downside to enabling the existing administrator account is that potential intruders have one foot in your digital door because they know the name of that account. You can close that door completely by changing the account name from Administrator to a new name that is not as obvious. In the Local Users and Groups window, right-click the administrator account, click Rename, and then type the new name.

continued ▶

Although you are free to add as many administrative-level accounts as you like, you should observe some caution when creating these accounts.

One of the main advantages to using an administrator account in Windows 8 is that it makes handling User Account Control prompts much easier. If you are running Windows 8 under a standard user account, when you attempt to change a system setting or install software, User Account Control prompts you to enter the username and password of an administrator account. Even if you know an administrator's logon credentials, it is still a hassle to have to enter this information each time. By contrast, when an administrator account attempts to change a setting or perform an installation, the user only needs to click OK to proceed.

This is much faster, but it places a great deal of power in the hands of the user. Therefore, before assigning an administrator account to any user, make sure the person understands the responsibilities and is familiar with User Account Control and how it works.

The New User dialog box appears.

③ Type the username.

④ Type the user's password in both text boxes.

⑤ Click User Must Change Password at Next Logon (☑ changes to ☐).

⑥ Click Create.

⑦ Click Close.

Ⓐ Windows 8 adds the new user to the Users folder.

⑧ Double-click the new user.

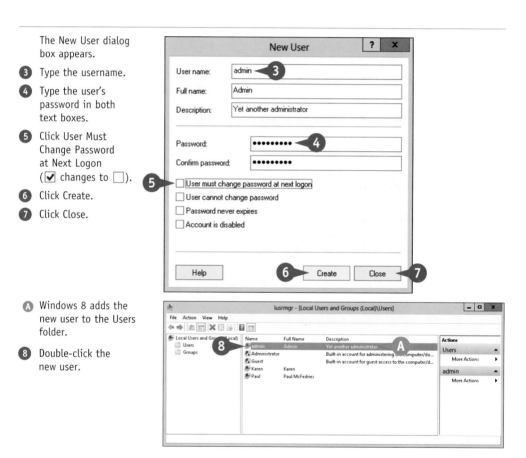

Windows 8 display's the user's Properties dialog box.

9 Click the Member Of tab.

10 Click Add.

The Select Groups dialog box appears.

11 Type **administrators**.

12 Click OK.

13 Click OK.

Windows 8 adds the new user to the Administrators group.

TIP

Important!
Whether you enable the built-in administrator account or add a new user to the administrators group, you should safeguard the account with a strong password. Such a password should be a minimum of eight characters long, and it should include at least one character from at least three of the following four sets: lowercase letters (a to z), uppercase letters (A to Z), numbers (0 to 9), and symbols (such as #, *, +, and _).

Activate the Guest User Account

You can give a visitor temporary and secure access to your computer or your network by letting that person log on using the built-in Windows 8 Guest account.

What do you do if you have someone visiting your home and that person wants to, for example, surf the web or access some media on your computer? You could allow the person to log on using an existing account, but that might not be reasonable because of privacy or security concerns. You could set up a separate user account for that person, but that is probably too

much work, particularly for a person on a short visit.

A better solution is to take advantage of the Guest account that comes with Windows 8. The Guest account is given only limited privileges, so anyone logged on under that account cannot access or edit your data, change computer settings, or install programs.

The Guest account is deactivated by default, so to allow your visitor to log on under that account, you must first activate it.

Enable the Guest Account

1 On the Start screen, type **lusrmgr.msc**.

2 Click lusrmgr in the search results.

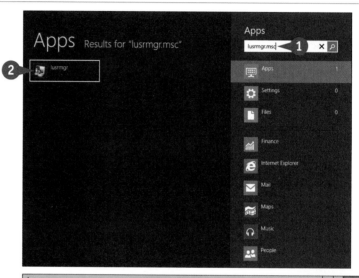

The Local Users and Groups window appears.

3 Click Users.

4 Double-click Guest.

The Guest Properties dialog box appears.

⑤ Click Account is Disabled (☑ changes to ☐).

⑥ Click OK.

Windows 8 activates the Guest account.

Log On to the Guest Account

① On the Start screen, click your user account tile.

② Click Guest.

TIPS

Secure It!

If you plan on leaving the Guest account activated for an extended time, you should secure it with a password. Type **lusrmgr.msc**, and press Enter. In the Local Users and Groups window, click Users, right-click Guest, and then click Set Password. In the Set Password for Guest dialog box, click Proceed, type the new password in the two text boxes, and then click OK.

Reverse It!

When you no longer need to use the Guest account, you should deactivate it again. To turn the Guest account off, follow steps 1 to 4 to open the Guest Properties dialog box. Click Account is Disabled (☐ changes to ☑), and then click OK. Windows 8 immediately deactivates the account.

Customize the Explorer Quick Access Toolbar

You can make File Explorer easier to use and more efficient by placing your most frequently used commands on the Quick Access Toolbar for one-click access.

The Windows 8 version of the venerable File Explorer file management program comes with a new ribbon interface that replaces the menu bar and toolbar in previous versions. As with all ribbons, the one in File Explorer is divided into several tabs: File, Home, Share, and View. This is a great way to expose all of the program's

functionality, but it can sometimes be hard to locate the command you want to use. Also, some commands take several clicks because you must first click the tab, drop down a list, and only then click the command.

If you have commands that you use frequently, you can put them within easy reach by adding them to the Quick Access Toolbar. Because the Quick Access Toolbar is always visible, any of its commands can be launched with just a single click.

Add a Default Command

1. Click the Customize Quick Access Toolbar arrow (▼).

2. Click the command you want to add.

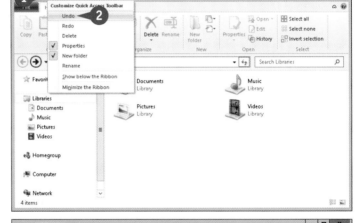

Ⓐ File Explorer adds the command to the Quick Access Toolbar.

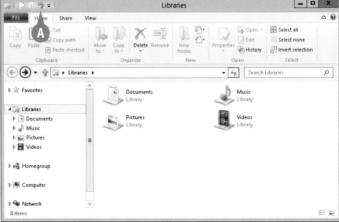

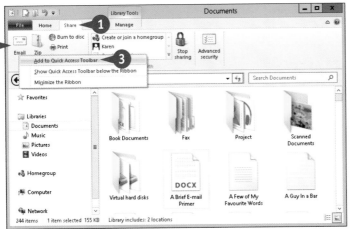

Add Any Ribbon Command

1. Click the tab that contains the command you want to add.

2. Right-click the command.

3. Click Add to Quick Access Toolbar.

Ⓑ File Explorer adds the command to the Quick Access Toolbar.

TIPS

More Options!
By default, the Quick Access Toolbar appears at the top of the File Explorer window in the title bar. Unfortunately, whenever File Explorer displays a Tools tab, it truncates the Quick Access Toolbar to show only seven icons. To work around this problem, right-click the Quick Access Toolbar and then click Show Quick Access Toolbar Below the Ribbon. This moves the toolbar below the ribbon, and so you always see all of its commands.

Remove It!
If you find that the Quick Access Toolbar is getting too crowded, or if you need to make room for another command, you can remove an existing command from the toolbar. To do this, right-click the command on the Quick Access Toolbar and then click Remove from Quick Access Toolbar.

49

Synchronize Settings between Multiple Devices

You can make Windows 8 easier to use, more consistent, and more efficient by synchronizing your settings, customizations, and data between multiple devices.

You can run Windows 8 using either a local user account or a Microsoft account. Using the latter enables you to store data online, connect social networks such as Facebook and Twitter, and access services such as the App Store and Music Store.

However, arguably the most useful feature of a Microsoft account is that you can use it to synchronize your settings across multiple

devices. If besides your Windows 8 desktop computer you also have a Windows 8 notebook, a Windows 8 tablet, and a Windows 8 phone, using the same Microsoft account on each device means you can synchronize data between them. You can sync customizations (such as backgrounds and themes), system settings (such as languages and regional settings), Internet Explorer data (such as favorites and history), app settings, and more. This gives you a consistent interface across your devices, and consistent data so you can be more productive.

---

① Move the mouse pointer to the top right corner of the screen.

Windows 8 displays the Charms menu.

Note: *You can also press Windows Logo+C. On a tablet, swipe in from the right edge to display the Charms menu.*

② Click Settings.

Windows 8 displays the Settings pane.

Note: *You can also display the Settings pane by pressing Windows Logo+I.*

③ Click Change PC Settings.

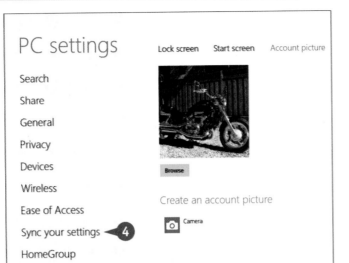

Windows 8 opens the PC Settings screen.

④ Click Sync Your Settings.

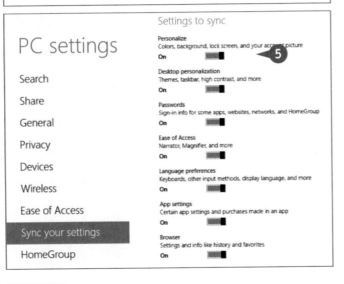

Windows 8 displays the Sync Your Settings screen.

⑤ Under Settings to Sync, click the switch to Off beside each type of settings that you do not want to include in the sync.

TIPS

More Options!

To configure Windows 8 to not sync when you use a metered Internet connection that only allows you so much data, follow steps 1 to 4 and click the Sync Settings Over Metered Connections switch to Off. To tell Windows 8 you are using a metered connection, press Windows Logo+I to open the Settings pane, click the network icon, right-click your Internet connection, and then click Set as Metered Connection.

Remove It!

In some cases, you might want the convenience of using a Microsoft account in Windows 8 for features such as the App Store and linked social networking accounts, but you do not want to synchronize settings and data. In that case, you can turn off synchronization for your computer altogether. Follow steps 1 to 4 to open the Sync Your Settings screen and then click the Sync Settings On this PC switch to Off.

Boosting Your Computer's Security and Privacy

Many security experts believe that most violations of security and privacy occur not remotely from the Internet, as you might expect, but locally, right at your computer. That is, computer security and privacy are compromised most often by someone simply sitting down at another person's machine while that person is not around. That makes some sense, because having physical access to a computer allows an intruder to install malicious programs, disable security features, and poke around for sensitive data, such as passwords and credit card numbers.

If you are worried about having your security or privacy compromised by someone having direct access to your computer, Windows 8 offers a reassuringly large number of tools and features that you can use to lock up your computer. In this chapter, you learn about most of these tools, many of which are simple to implement. Techniques such as activating parental controls, adding a picture password to your account, automatically locking your computer, and clearing your personal information from the Start screen are all easy to set up, but provide greatly enhanced security and privacy. You also learn more advanced techniques that take security to the next level, including using advanced file permissions and preventing other people from even starting your computer.

Switch to Advanced Sharing to Improve Security

If you share files with other network users, you can configure Windows 8 to control which users can access your files and what actions they can perform on those files.

If your computer is part of a network, it is common to give other users access to some of your files by sharing one or more folders with the network. By default, Windows 8 runs the Sharing Wizard when you opt to share a folder. The Sharing Wizard enables you to choose which users can share the folder and how each person

shares it: with Read/Write permissions (the user can make changes) or with Read permissions (the user cannot make changes).

If you want to apply more sophisticated sharing options such as the folder permissions discussed in the next section, you need to switch to the Windows 8 advanced sharing features. These features enable you to set permissions for specific users and for groups of users (such as Administrators or Guests), create multiple shares for the same folder, and more.

① On the Start screen, type **control**.

② Click Control Panel.

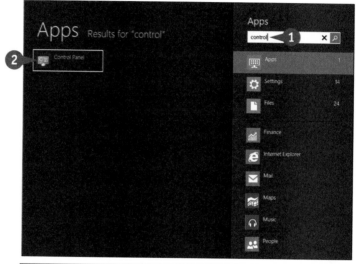

The Control Panel window appears.

③ Click Appearance and Personalization.

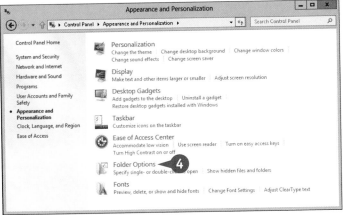

The Appearance and Personalization window appears.

④ Click Folder Options.

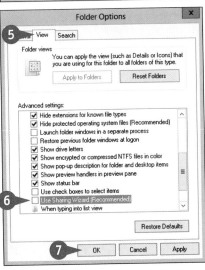

The Folder Options dialog box appears.

⑤ Click the View tab.

⑥ Click the Use Sharing Wizard check box (☑ changes to ☐).

⑦ Click OK.

Windows 8 switches to its advanced sharing options.

Protect a File or Folder with Permissions

Windows 8 offers a sophisticated file security system called permissions. *Permissions* specify exactly what the groups or users can do with the contents of a protected folder. There are six types of permissions.

With **Full Control** permission, users can perform any of the actions listed. Users can also change permissions. With **Modify** permission, users can view the folder contents, open files, edit files, create new files and subfolders, delete files, and run programs. With **Read & Execute** permission, users can view the folder contents, open files, and run programs. With **List Folder Contents** permission, users can view the folder contents. With **Read** permission, users can open files, but cannot edit them. Finally, with **Write** permission, users can create new files and subfolders and open and edit existing files.

In each case, you can either allow the permission or deny it.

---

① In File Explorer, click the folder or file that you want to protect.

② Click the Home tab.

③ Click Properties.

Note: *You can also right-click the folder or file and then click Properties.*

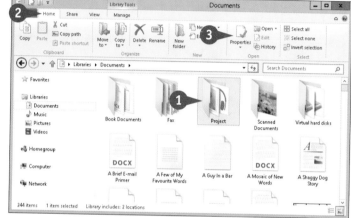

The item's Properties dialog box appears.

④ Click the Security tab.

Ⓐ The Group or User Names list displays the current groups and users that have permissions for the folder.

Note: *In some cases, the name in parentheses takes the form COMPUTER\Name, where COMPUTER is the computer's name and Name is the user or group name.*

⑤ Click Edit.

The Permissions dialog box appears.

⑥ Click Add.

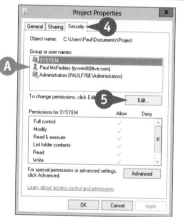

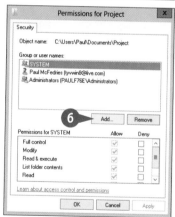

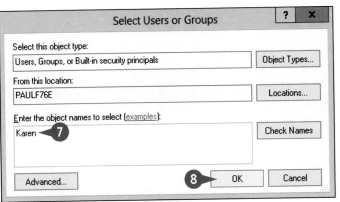

The Select Users or Groups dialog box appears.

⑦ Type the name of the group or user you want to work with.

⑧ Click OK.

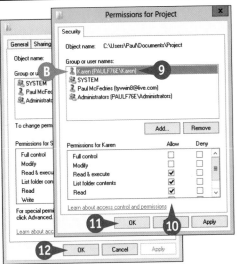

Ⓑ The user or group appears in this list.

⑨ Click the new user or group to select it.

⑩ In the Allow column, click each permission that you want to allow (☐ changes to ☑).

⑪ Click OK.

⑫ Click OK.

Windows 8 protects the folder with the permissions you selected.

More Options!

In the Select Users or Groups dialog box, if you are not sure about a user or group name, click Advanced and then click Find Now. Windows 8 displays a list of all the available users and groups. Click the name you want in the list and then click OK.

More Options!

You can override a user's group permissions by clicking the corresponding check boxes in the Deny column (☐ changes to ☑). For example, to prevent a member of the Administrators group from viewing the contents of your folder, click the List Folder Contents in the Deny column check box (☐ changes to ☑).

Clear Personal Data from the Start Screen

To enhance your privacy, you can clear the Start screen's personal data so that other people who use your computer cannot see your private information.

Many of the Start screen's tiles display personal information. For example, the People tile shows recent updates, the Messaging and Mail tiles show recent messages, and the Photos, Music, and Video tiles show currently playing media. However, if you know that someone else is going to be using your computer, and you do not have a separate user account set up for that person, you may not want him or her to see this

information. To prevent this, you can clear all your personal data from the Start screen's tiles.

However, the Start screen is not the only place where Windows 8 stores your personal data. Windows Media Player maintains a list of files that you have played recently, and it also keeps track of the addresses of Internet media you have recently opened, as well as all the information you have downloaded about the audio CDs and DVDs you played. If someone else is going to use Windows Media Player on your computer, you can maintain your media privacy by clearing all this stored information.

1 Display the Start screen.

2 Press Windows Logo+I.

The Settings pane appears.

3 Click Tiles.

The Start Settings pane appears.

④ Click Clear.

Ⓐ Windows 8 removes all your personal data from the Start screen tiles.

TIPS

More Options!

To clear your recent media, open Windows Media Player, click Organize, and then click Options to open the Options dialog box. Click the Privacy tab. Click Clear History to clear the list of recently viewed media files and Internet addresses. Click Clear Caches to clear the downloaded information about audio CDs. Click OK.

Did You Know?

The easiest way to maintain the privacy of your documents is to create separate user accounts for each person who uses your computer. Press Windows Logo+I, click Change PC Settings, click Users, and then click Add a User. For maximum privacy and security, Windows 8 makes each new user a Standard user with limited permissions.

Turn Off Recent App Switching

If another person is going to be using your computer, or if you will be leaving your computer unattended for a period of time, you can disable the recent app switching list so another person cannot see the apps you have used recently.

When you use Windows 8 apps, the system maintains a list of apps you have recently used. This enables you to switch between those apps by displaying the recent apps list. That is, you place the mouse pointer in the top left corner of

the screen and then move the pointer down (or press Windows Logo+Tab), and then click the thumbnail of the app you want to use next. With a tablet, you can slide your finger in from the left edge of the screen to switch to the next app in the list.

If you do not want anyone else to know which apps you have used recently, you can turn off recent app switching. This disables the recent apps list and prevents tablet users from bringing recent apps onto the screen.

---

1 Press Windows Logo+I.

A The Settings pane appears.

2 Click Change PC Settings.

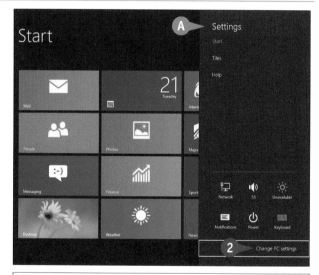

The PC Settings app appears.

3 Click General.

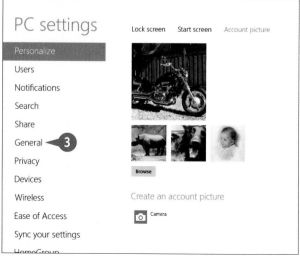

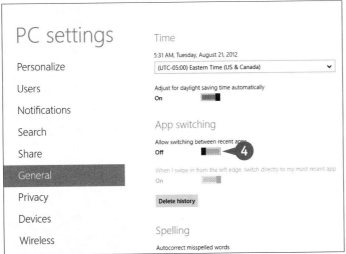

The General settings appear.

④ Click the Allow Switching Between Recent Apps switch to Off.

Ⓑ When you move the mouse pointer to the top left corner of the screen, the recent apps list no longer appears.

Also, pressing Windows Logo+Tab no longer displays a list of running apps.

Try This!

If another person is going to be using your computer, turning off recent app switching protects your privacy, but it makes Windows 8 more difficult for the other person to use. Rather than turning off recent app switching altogether, you can just delete your recent app history, instead. Follow steps 1 to 3 to display the General settings, and then click Delete History. This leaves recent app switching activated, but it means that the other person creates a fresh list of recent apps.

Configure Action Center Messages

You can make your computer more secure by ensuring that Action Center is configured to display all of its security and maintenance messages.

If you are working in the Windows 8 Desktop app and Windows detects a problem, the Action Center uses the taskbar's notification area to display a message that alerts you to the issue. These messages fall into two categories: security and maintenance.

Security messages include letting you know if your computer does not have any virus or spyware protection, if the virus or spyware

protection is out of date, if Windows Update is turned off, and if your Internet security settings are not as strong as they should be.

Maintenance messages include alerting you to a failed backup, telling you if a drive is running out of space, and letting you know if automatic maintenance has been turned off.

These are useful messages, but it is fairly easy to turn them off. To ensure all your computers are fully protected, you should periodically check to make sure all security and maintenance messages are being displayed.

---

① Press Windows Logo+W.

The Settings search pane appears.

② Type **action**.

③ Click Action Center.

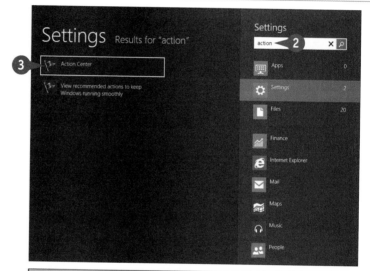

Windows 8 opens the Action Center window.

④ Click Change Action Center Settings.

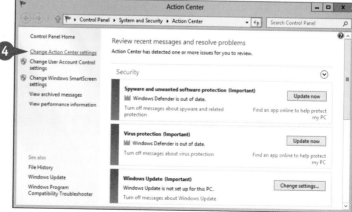

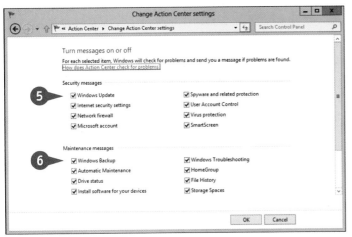

The Change Action Center Settings window appears.

⑤ Click to activate each item in the Security Messages section (☐ changes to ☑).

⑥ Click to activate each item in the Maintenance Messages section (☐ changes to ☑).

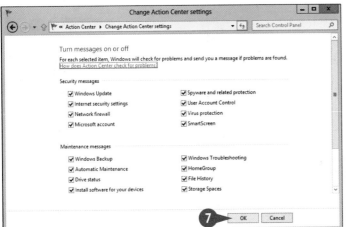

⑦ Click OK.

Windows 8 puts the new Action Center message settings into effect.

TIPS

Did You Know?

To view your current Action Center messages, follow steps 1 to 3 to open the Action Center window. Click Security to expand that section and display its most recent messages in each category (Virus Protection, Windows Update, and so on). Click Maintenance to expand that section and display its most recent messages in each category (Automatic Maintenance, Drive Status, File History, and so on).

Did You Know?

You can view older Action Center messages, as well. To do this, follow steps 1 to 3 to open the Action Center window, and then click the View Archived Messages link. When you have finished viewing the messages, click OK to return to Action Center.

Configure User Account Control Settings

You can configure the Windows 8 user account control (UAC) to suit the way you work.

The basic idea behind the UAC security model is to prevent harmful programs such as viruses and Trojan horses from installing themselves on your PC and changing your system settings. It does this by monitoring your system for four types of events: a program initiating a software install, a program changing system settings, a user changing system settings, and a user running high-level Windows 8 tools such as the Registry Editor.

If you are coming to Windows 8 from Windows Vista, you are used to UAC prompting you for permission to perform any of these events, which meant you probably ended up supplying Windows

with administrator credentials quite often. This is known as *elevating* your privileges. Also, when prompting for credentials, Windows Vista would switch to *secure desktop mode*, which meant that you could not do anything else with Windows Vista until you either supplied your credentials or cancelled the operation.

In Windows 7 (and continuing in Windows 8), Microsoft tweaked UAC to make it configurable so you can tailor the prompts to suit your situation. Microsoft also set up the default configuration of UAC so that it now only rarely prompts you for elevation when you change the settings on your PC.

---

1. Press Windows Logo+W.

   The Settings search screen appears.

2. Type **account control**.

3. Click Change User Account Control Settings.

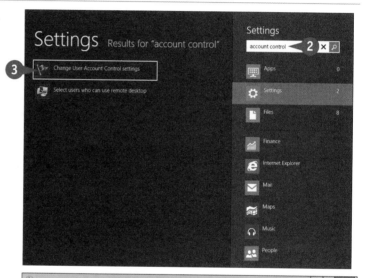

The User Account Control Settings window appears.

4. Click and drag the slider to choose one of the four UAC settings.

A. This box displays a brief description of each level.

Note: *See the tip to learn more about each setting.*

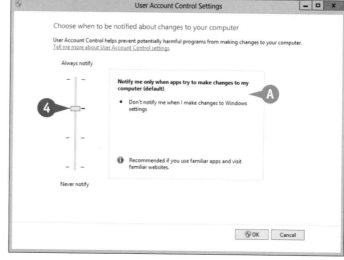

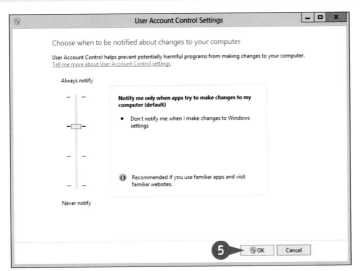

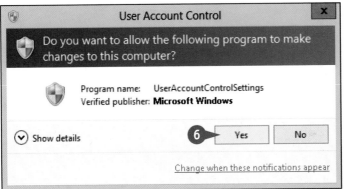

5 Click OK.

The User Account Control dialog box appears.

6 Click Yes.

Note: *If you are not currently using an administrator account, you must provide the password for an administrator account on your system.*

Windows 8 applies the new UAC setting.

TIP

Did You Know?
The top level (Always Notify) works much like UAC in Windows Vista because you are prompted for elevation when you change Windows settings and when programs try to change settings and install software. The second highest level is the default setting, and it prompts you for elevation only when programs try to change settings and install software. This level uses secure desktop mode to display the UAC dialog box.

The second lowest level is the same as the Default level — that is, it prompts you for elevations only when programs try to change settings and install software — but this level does not use secure desktop mode when displaying the UAC dialog box. The lowest level (Never Notify) turns off UAC.

Require Ctrl+Alt+Delete Before Signing In

You can configure Windows 8 to require users to press Ctrl+Alt+Delete before they can sign in to your computer. This prevents a malicious program activated at startup from capturing your password.

Although your Windows 8 user account is protected with a password, it is not foolproof. Hackers are an endlessly resourceful bunch, and some of the smarter ones have figured out a way to defeat the user account password system. The trick is that they install a virus or Trojan horse program — usually via an infected e-mail

message or malicious website — that loads itself when you start your computer. This program then displays a *fake* version of the Windows 8 sign on screen. When you type your username and password into this dialog box, the program records it and your system security is compromised.

To thwart this clever ruse, Windows 8 enables you to configure your system so that you must press Ctrl+Alt+Delete before you can sign in. This key combination ensures that the authentic sign on screen appears.

1 Press Windows Logo+R.

The Run dialog box appears.

2 In the Open text box, type **control userpasswords2**.

3 Click OK.

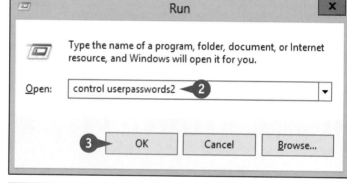

The User Accounts dialog box appears.

4 Click the Users tab.

5 Click the Users Must Enter a User Name and Password to Use This Computer check box (☐ changes to ☑).

6 Click the Advanced tab.

7 Click the Require Users to Press Ctrl+Alt+Delete check box (☐ changes to ☑).

8 Click OK.

Windows 8 now requires each user to press Ctrl+Alt+Delete to sign in.

Ⓐ At the next sign on, Windows 8 displays this message in the lock screen.

TIP

Did You Know?

When you are signed in to Windows 8, you can use Ctrl+Alt+Delete to sign out or switch to a different user account from any part of Windows (not just the Start screen, where you access these features by clicking your user account tile). Press Ctrl+Alt+Delete to display the Windows Security screen. If you want to sign out of your account, click Sign Out. If you prefer to stay signed in and switch to a different account, click Switch User instead.

You can also use this key combination as a quick way to launch Task Manager from the Start screen. That is, rather than running a search for Task Manager, you can press Ctrl+Alt+Delete and then click Task Manager in the Windows Security screen.

Lock Your Computer to Prevent Others from Using It

You can lock your computer to prevent another person from working with your computer while you are away from your desk.

Security measures such as advanced file permissions and encryption, which are covered in this chapter, rely on the fact that you have entered the appropriate username and password to sign in to your Windows 8 account. In other words, after you sign in, you become a "trusted" user.

But what happens when you leave your desk? If you remain signed in to Windows 8, any other person who sits down at your computer can take advantage of your trusted-user status to view and work with secure files. You could prevent this by shutting down your computer every time you leave your desk, but that is not practical. A better solution is to lock your system before leaving your desk. Anyone who tries to use your computer must enter your password to access the Windows 8 desktop.

To learn more about how to configure Windows 8 to lock your computer after it has been idle for a while, see the next section.

Lock Your Computer

1 On the Start screen, click your user account tile.

2 Click Lock.

The Windows 8 lock screen appears.

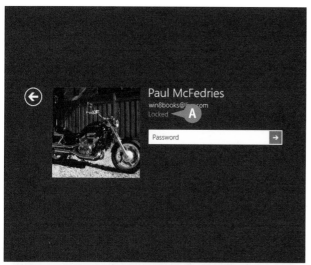

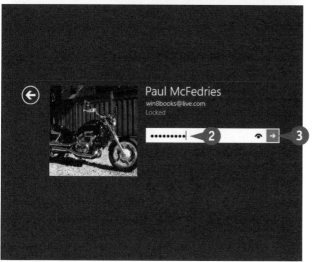

Unlock Your Computer

1 Press a key.

The Windows 8 sign on screen appears.

Note: *On a tablet, swipe the lock screen up to reveal the sign on screen.*

A The word Locked appears below your username.

2 Type your password.

3 Click the Submit arrow or press Enter.

The Windows 8 desktop appears.

TIPS

Did You Know?

If you need to leave your desk in a hurry, Windows 8 offers a couple of quick methods for locking your computer. Probably the quickest way is to press the Windows Logo+L keys. Alternatively, press Ctrl+Alt+Delete and then click Lock.

Try This!

If you want a one-click method for locking your computer, right-click the desktop, click New, click Shortcut, and then type the following: **rundll32 user32.dll,LockWorkStation**. Click Next, type **Lock**, and then click Finish. Drag the new shortcut and drop it on the taskbar. Right-click the shortcut and then click Pin to Start. You can now click the pinned taskbar icon or Start screen tile to lock your PC.

Automatically Lock Your Computer

You can configure Windows 8 to automatically lock your computer after it has been idle for a specified time.

The previous section described how to lock your computer to prevent an intruder from accessing your desktop while you are away from your PC. The locking technique is easy enough to do, but the hard part is *remembering* to do it. If you are late for a meeting or other appointment, locking

up your machine is probably the last thing on your mind as you dash out the door. If you later remember that you forgot to lock your computer, you may spend the next while worrying about your PC.

To avoid the worrying and to reduce the chance that some snoop will access your desktop if you forget to lock it, you can configure Windows 8 to lock automatically after a period of inactivity.

---

① On the Start screen, type **control**.

② Click Control Panel.

The Control Panel window appears.

③ Click Change the Theme.

The Personalization window appears.

Note: *A quicker way to get to the Personalization window is to press Windows Logo+W, type **personalize**, and then click Personalize Your Computer.*

④ Click Screen Saver.

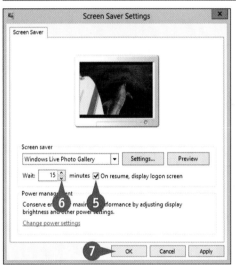

⑤ Click On Resume, Display Logon Screen (☐ changes to ☑).

⑥ Use the Wait spin box to set the number of minutes of idle that must pass before Windows 8 locks your computer.

⑦ Click OK.

Windows 8 now automatically locks your PC when it has been idle for the number of minutes you specified in step 6.

TIP

Check It Out!

Windows 8 is also configured by default to display the sign on screen when your computer wakes up from sleep mode. To make sure this setting is activated, follow steps 1 and 2 to open the Control Panel window. Click Hardware and Sound, and then under Power Options, click Require a Password When the Computer Wakes.

In the System Settings window, examine the options in the Password Protection on Wakeup section. If the Don't Require a Password option is activated, click Change Settings That Are Currently Unavailable to enable the options. (You may need to enter administrator credentials at this point.) Click the Require a Password option (○ changes to ◉), and then click Save Changes.

Prevent Others from Starting Your Computer

You can configure Windows 8 to require a special media to be inserted in your computer before starting up. Without the media, Windows 8 does not allow anyone to sign in to the computer.

As a security feature, Windows 8 stores passwords in encrypted form and Windows 8 uses a system key to decrypt the passwords. This system key is normally stored on your computer, and if for some reason the system key were lost, you would not be able to start your computer. For this reason, the system key is also called a startup key.

You can take advantage of this security precaution to make sure that no unauthorized

user can start your computer. You do that by having Windows 8 move the startup key to a removable media such as a USB flash drive. If the media is not inserted into the computer at startup, Windows 8 does not allow anyone to sign in to the system. In fact, Windows 8 does not even display the sign on screen, so an unauthorized user cannot even try to guess your password.

You must first configure your removable media to use drive A, so see "Assign a Different Letter to a Disk Drive" in Chapter 4.

---

① Insert a removable drive, such as a USB flash drive, into your computer, and configure it to use drive A.

② On the Start screen, type **command**.

③ Right-click Command Prompt.

④ Click Run as Administrator.

Note: *You can also press Windows Logo+X and then click Command Prompt (Admin).*

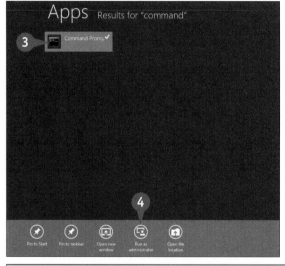

Note: *If you see the User Account Control dialog box, click Yes or enter administrator credentials.*

The Command Prompt window appears.

⑤ Type **syskey**.

⑥ Press Enter.

⑦ Click Close to shut down the Command Prompt window.

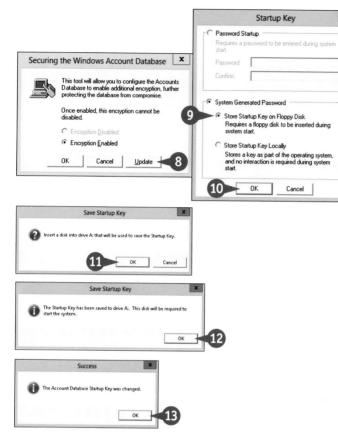

The Securing the Windows Account Database dialog box appears.

⑧ Click Update.

The Startup Key dialog box appears.

⑨ Click the Store Startup Key on Floppy Disk option (○ changes to ◉).

⑩ Click OK.

The Save Startup Key dialog box appears.

⑪ Click OK.

Windows 8 saves the startup key to the removable drive and then displays a confirmation dialog box.

⑫ Click OK.

The Success dialog box appears.

⑬ Click OK.

Windows 8 now requires the removable drive that contains the startup key to be inserted each time you sign in.

TIPS

Caution!

After saving the startup key to the removable drive, Windows 8 looks for the drive when you start your computer. If Windows 8 does not find the key, the Windows 8 Startup Key Disk dialog box appears. You must insert the drive and then click OK. If you lose or damage the drive, you cannot start Windows 8, so keep the drive in a safe place. Also, be sure to make a backup copy of the drive.

Remove It!

If you decide later on that you no longer want to keep the startup key on a floppy disk, you can revert to storing the key on your computer. Follow steps 1 to 8, click the Store Startup Key Locally option (○ changes to ◉), and then click OK. Insert the removable drive that has the startup key, and then click OK.

Create a Picture Password

You can make it much easier to sign in to your Windows 8 tablet by creating a picture password.

If you are serious about your tablet's security, then you should have configured your Windows 8 user account with a strong password. This means a password that is at least eight characters long, and uses at least one character from at least three of the following four sets: lowercase letters, uppercase letters, numbers, and symbols. However, the stronger the password you use, the more cumbersome it is to enter using a touch keyboard.

If you find that it is taking you an inordinate amount of time to sign in to Windows 8 using your tablet's touch keyboard, you can switch to a picture password, instead. In this case, your "password" is a series of three gestures — any combination of a tap, a straight line, or a circle — that you apply to a photo. Windows 8 displays the photo at startup, and you repeat your gestures, in order, to sign in to Windows.

① Using your tablet, swipe left from the right edge and then tap Search (not shown).

② Type **password**.

③ Tap Create or Change Picture Password.

The PC Settings app appears.

④ Tap Create a Picture Password.

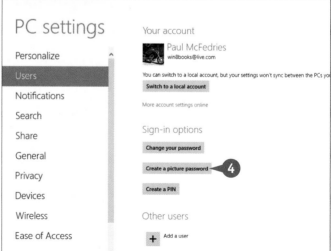

Windows 8 prompts you for your account password.

⑤ Type your password.

⑥ Tap OK.

The Welcome to Picture Password screen appears.

⑦ Tap Choose Picture.

TIPS

Caution!
The biggest drawback to using a picture password is that it is possible for a malicious user to view and possibly even record your gestures using a camera. Unlike a regular text password where the characters appear as dots to prevent someone from seeing them, your gestures have no such protection.

Important!
Remember that your picture password is applied to your user account along with your existing text-based password. That is, the picture password does *not* replace your text password. As you see in the continuation of this section, it is trivial to bypass the picture password and sign in using the text password, so it is vital that you still protect your tablet with a strong text password.

continued ▶

In the same way that you should not choose a regular account password that is extremely obvious (such as the word "password" or your username), you should take care to avoid creating an obvious picture password.

For example, if you are using a photo showing three faces, then an obvious picture password would be a tap on each face.

A good picture password not only uses all three available gestures, but also uses them in ways that are not obvious.

To ensure you have memorized your picture password, you should practice signing out from your account and then signing back on using the picture password a few times.

The Files screen appears.

8 Tap the picture you want to use.

9 Tap Open.

The How's This Look? screen appears.

10 Tap and drag the picture so that the image is positioned where you prefer.

11 Tap Use this Picture.

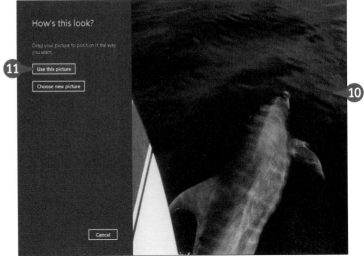

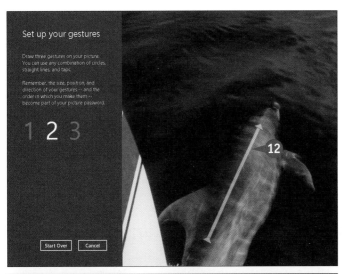

The Set Up Your Gestures screen appears.

⑫ Use your finger or a stylus to draw three gestures.

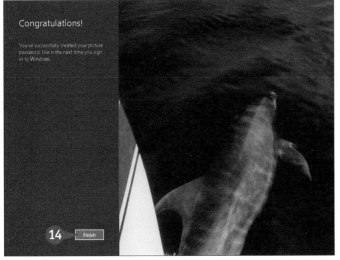

⑬ Repeat the gestures to confirm.

⑭ Tap Finish.

The next time you sign in to Windows 8, you will be prompted to enter your picture password gestures.

TIPS

Important!

If you forget the gestures in your picture password, tap Switch to Password in the sign on screen to sign in with your regular password. To get a reminder of your picture password gestures, follow steps 1 to 3, tap Change Picture Password, type your user account password, and tap OK. In the Change Your Picture Password screen, tap Replay. Tap the picture to see each gesture.

Change It!

If you feel that your picture password has been compromised (for example, someone witnessed your sign on), if you want to change your gestures, or if you have grown tired of the original picture you chose, you can change your picture password. Open the Change Picture Password screen as described in the previous tip, choose a new picture, if necessary, and then run through your gestures.

Getting More Out of Files and Folders

Although you may use Windows 8 to achieve certain ends — write memos and letters, create presentations, play games, surf the Internet, and so on — you still have to deal with files and folders as part of your day-to-day work or play. Basic tasks such as copying and moving files, creating and renaming folders, and deleting unneeded files and folders are part of the Windows 8 routine.

Your goal should be to make all this file and folder maintenance *less* of a routine so that you have more time during the day to devote to more worthy pursuits. Fortunately, Windows 8 offers a number of shortcuts and tweaks that can speed up file and

folder tasks and make them more efficient. In this chapter you learn a number of these techniques.

For example, you learn how to display file extensions, how to open a file in a program other than the one with which it is associated, how to store your file history on a USB drive, how to revert to a previous version of a file, and how to protect a file by making it read-only. You also learn how to mount an ISO file and virtual hard disk, how to combine multiple drives into a single storage pool, how to assign a different letter to a disk drive, how to hide drive letters, and how to split a hard drive into two partitions.

Turn On File Extensions

You can make files easier to understand and work with by configuring Windows 8 to display file extensions.

A *file extension* is a code of three (or sometimes four or more) characters that appears at the end of a filename, after the period. For example, in the filename readme.txt, the "txt" part is the file extension. Windows 8 uses file extensions to determine a document's file type. For example, a file with a txt extension is a Text Document type, whereas a file with a bmp extension is a Bitmap Image type.

In Windows 8, each file type is associated with a particular application: Text Document files are associated with Notepad, Bitmap Image files are associated with Windows Photo Viewer, and so on. So file extensions are important because they determine a document's file type and the application that opens the document.

Windows 8 ships with file extensions turned off. This is often a problem because it is difficult to tell what file type a document uses without seeing the extension. Also, with file extensions hidden, you cannot change the extension to something else.

 Open a folder window.

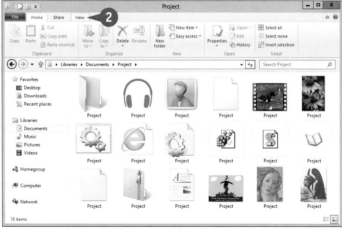 Click the View tab.

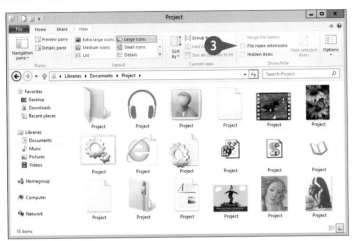

③ Click File Name Extensions (☐ changes to ☑).

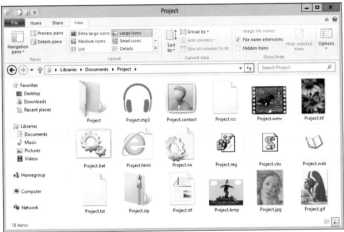

Windows 8 now displays file extensions.

Did You Know?

Windows 8 ships with file extensions turned off because it does not want novice users imprudently changing extensions and possibly rendering documents unusable. However, changing file extensions has many uses. For example, if you use Notepad to create a web page, the resulting file uses the .txt extension, but most web page files must use either the .htm or .html extension, so you must change it.

Apply It!

Once you have configured Windows 8 to display file extensions, you can then edit a file's extension. To do this, use File Explorer to navigate to the folder containing the file, click the file, and then press F2. Windows 8 displays a text box around the filename and selects the part of the name to the left of the dot (.). Press the right arrow key to collapse the selection and move the cursor into the extension. Note that Windows 8 will ask you to confirm the extension change.

Specify a Different Program When Opening a File

You can open a file in a different program from the one normally associated with the file. This enables you to use the other program's features to work on the file.

Every document you create has a particular file type. Some file types include Text Documents, Rich Text Documents, Bitmap Images, and JPEG Images. All these types have a default program associated with them. For example, Text Documents are associated with Notepad, and Rich Text Documents are associated with

WordPad or Word. Double-clicking a file opens the file in the associated program.

You may have situations where you prefer to open a particular file with a different program. For example, double-clicking a picture file opens it in the Windows Photo Viewer. However, you may prefer to open the picture file in Paint or some other image-editing program so that you can make changes to the picture.

This section shows you how to open any document in another program.

---

① Open the folder that contains the file you want to open.

② Click the file.

③ Click the Open list.

Ⓐ If the program you want to use appears here, click the program and skip the remaining steps.

④ Click Choose Default Program.

Windows 8 asks how you want to open this file type.

⑤ Click More Options.

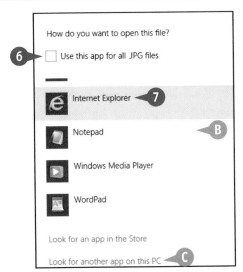

Ⓑ Windows 8 displays a full list of programs you can use to open the file.

⑥ Click to deselect the Use This App for All *.ext* Files check box, where *ext* is the extension of the file (☑ changes to ☐).

⑦ Click the program you want to use to open the file.

Ⓒ If the program you want to use does not appear in the list, you can click Look for Another App on This PC and use the Open With dialog box to specify the program.

Windows 8 opens the file in the program you chose.

Store File History on an External Drive

You can make it easier to recover earlier versions of your files by saving copies of your files to an external drive.

You know that you can back up any file by copying it to another drive. However, there may be times when it is not good enough just to store a copy of a file. For example, if you make frequent changes to a file, you might want to copy not only the current version, but also the versions from an hour ago, a day ago, a week ago, and so on. In Windows 8, these previous versions of a file are called its *file history*, and you can save this data for all your documents by activating a feature called File History.

When you turn on File History and specify an external drive to store the data, Windows 8 begins monitoring your libraries, your desktop, your contacts, and your Internet Explorer favorites. Once an hour, Windows 8 checks to see if any of this data has changed since the last check. If it has, Windows 8 saves copies of the changed files to the external drive.

Once you have some data saved, you can then use it to restore a previous version of a file, as described later in this chapter.

Set the File History Drive

1 Connect an external drive to your PC.

Note: *The drive should have enough capacity to hold your files, so an external hard drive is probably best.*

2 On the Start screen, press Windows Logo+W.

The Settings search pane appears.

3 Type **history**.

4 Click File History.

The File History window appears.

A If Windows 8 detects an external hard drive, it displays the drive here.

If this is the correct drive, you can skip steps 5 to 7.

5 Click Select Drive.

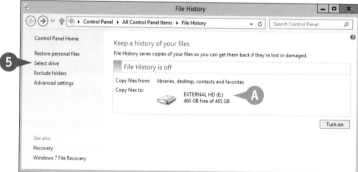

The Select Drive window appears.

6 Click the drive you want to use.

7 Click OK.

Activate File History

1 Click Turn On.

Windows 8 activates File History and begins saving copies of your files to the external drive.

More Options!
If you do not have an external drive, or if your drives do not have enough capacity, you can use a network folder to store your file history. In the File History window, either click the Use Network Location link, or click Select Drive and then click Add Network Location. In the Select Folder dialog box, open a computer on your network, select a shared folder to which you have permission to add files, and then click Select Folder.

Remove It!
If you need to remove the external drive temporarily (for example, if you need to use the port for another device), you should turn off File History before disconnecting the external drive. Follow steps 1 to 4 to open the File History window and then click Turn Off.

Exclude a Folder from Your File History

You can make the File History feature more convenient or more secure by preventing certain folders from being copied to the drive.

By default, File History stores copies of everything in your Windows 8 libraries — including Documents, Music, Photos, and Videos — as well as your desktop items, contacts, and Internet Explorer favorites. However, there may be situations where you do not want every file to be included in your history. For example, if

your external drive has a limited capacity, you might want to exclude extremely large files, such as TV shows or movies in your Videos library.

Similarly, you might have sensitive or private files in your Documents library that you do not want to copy to the external drive because that drive can easily be stolen or lost.

Whatever the reason, you can configure File History to exclude a particular folder from being copied to the external drive.

① Open the File History window as described in the previous section.

② Click Exclude Folders.

The Exclude Folders window appears.

③ Click Add.

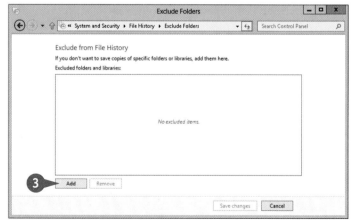

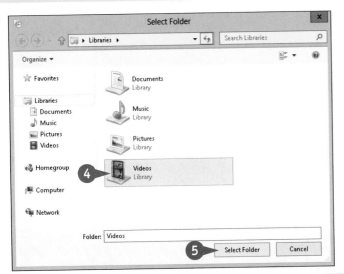

The Select Folder dialog box appears.

④ Click the folder you want to exclude.

⑤ Click Select Folder.

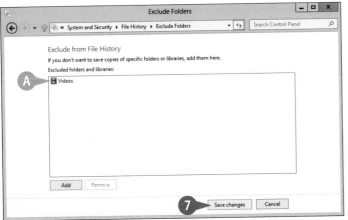

Ⓐ Windows 8 adds the folder to the Excluded Folders and Libraries list.

⑥ Repeat steps 3 to 5 to exclude any other folders you do not want in your file history.

⑦ Click Save Changes.

Windows 8 no longer includes files from the folder in your file history.

TIPS

More Options!

By default, File History looks for changed files every hour. If you are particularly busy, you might prefer a more frequent save interval. On the other hand, if you are running out of space on the external drive, you might prefer a less frequent save interval to preserve space. In the File History window, click Advanced Settings and then use the Save Copies of Files list to select the save frequency you prefer.

Did You Know?

File History does not delete any of the file versions it saves. To free up space on the external drive, you can configure File History to save versions after a while. Click Advanced Settings and then use the Keep Saved Versions list to choose the time interval you want to use.

Restore a Previous Version of a File

If you improperly edit, accidentally delete, or corrupt a file through a system crash, in many cases you can restore a previous version of the file.

When you activate File History on your PC as described earlier in this chapter, Windows 8 periodically — by default, once an hour — looks for files that have changed since the last check. If it finds a changed file, it makes a copy of that file and saves that version of the file to the external drive that you specified when you set up File History. This gives Windows 8 the capability to reverse the changes you have made

to a file by reverting to an earlier state of the file. An earlier state of a file is called a *previous version*.

Why would you want to revert to a previous version of a file? One reason is that you might improperly edit the file by deleting or changing important data. In some cases you may be able to restore that data by going back to a previous version of the file. Another reason is that the file might become corrupted if the program or Windows 8 crashes. You can get a working version of the file back by restoring to a previous version.

---

① On the Start screen, press Windows Logo+W.

The Settings search pane appears.

② Type **history**.

③ Click File History.

The File History window appears.

④ Click Restore Personal Files.

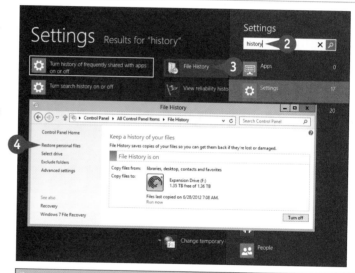

The Home - File History window appears.

⑤ Double-click the library that contains the file you want to restore.

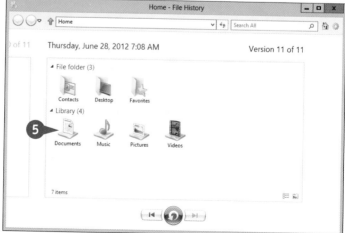

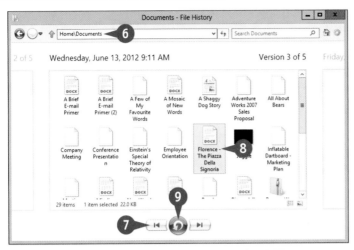

6 Open the folder that contains the file.

7 Click Previous Version until you open the version of the folder you want to use.

8 Click the file you want to restore.

9 Click Restore to Original Location.

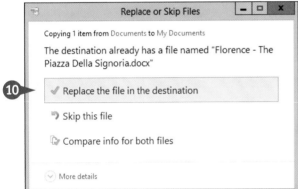

If the original folder has a file with the same name, File History asks what you want to do.

10 Select an option:

Click Replace the File in the Destination to overwrite the existing file with the previous version.

Click Skip This File to do nothing.

Click Compare Info for Both Files to decide which file you prefer to keep.

Windows 8 restores the previous version.

TIPS

Did You Know?

Windows 8 also keeps track of previous versions of folders, which is useful if an entire folder becomes corrupted because of a system crash. Follow steps 1 to 7, click the folder you want to restore, and then click Restore to Original Location.

More Options!

If you are not sure whether to replace an existing file with a previous version, click Compare Info for Both Files in the Replace or Skip Files dialog box. In the File Conflict dialog box, activate the check box beside both versions (☐ changes to ☑), and then click Continue. This leaves the existing file as is and restores the previous version with (2) appended to the filename.

Protect a File by Making It Read-Only

You can prevent other people from making changes to an important file by designating the file as read-only.

A lot of day-to-day work in Windows 8 is required but not terribly important. Most memos, letters, and notes are run-of-the-mill and do not require extra security. Occasionally, however, you may create or work with a file that *is* important. It could be a carefully crafted letter, a memo detailing an important company strategy, or a collection of hard-won brainstorming notes. Whatever the content, such a file requires extra protection to ensure that you do not lose your work.

You can set advanced file permissions that can prevent a document from being changed or even deleted (see "Protect a File or Folder with Permissions" in Chapter 3). If your only concern is preventing other people from making changes to a document, a simpler technique you can use is making the document *read-only*. This means that although other people can make changes to the document, they cannot *save* those changes (except to a new file). This section shows you how to make a file read-only.

Make a File Read-Only

1. Open the folder that contains the file you want to work with.

2. Click the file.

3. Click the Home tab.

4. Click the top half of the Properties button.

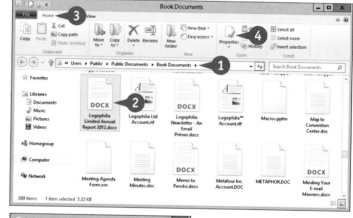

The file's Properties dialog box appears.

5. Click the General tab.

6. Click the Read-only check box (☐ changes to ☑).

7. Click OK.

The file is now read-only.

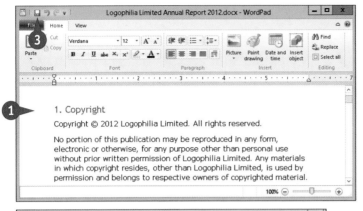

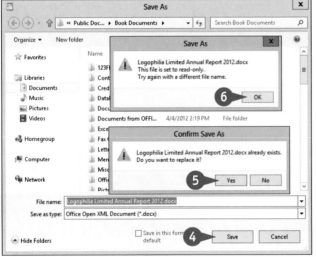

Confirm That a File Is Read-Only

1. Open the read-only file.

2. Make changes to the file.

3. Click Save or press Ctrl+S.

The Save As dialog box appears.

4. Click Save.

The Confirm Save As dialog box appears.

5. Click Yes.

The program tells you the file is read-only.

6. Click OK.

Restore Folder Windows When You Log On

You can make many desktop chores easier and more efficient if you configure Windows 8 to reopen at logon any folder windows that you left open when you last signed out.

Unfortunately, the presence of the new user interface in Windows 8 does not mean you never again have to deal with files and folders. In fact, you will likely find yourself using the Windows 8 Desktop app quite often for file and folder maintenance chores.

You cannot escape those chores, but you can make them easier. In particular, if you have

several folder windows that you routinely open when you first launch the Desktop app, reopening those windows every time is time-consuming and wasteful. You can avoid that waste and save yourself some time by getting Windows 8 to open the windows automatically. Specifically, you can configure Windows 8 to remember any folder windows you had open when you signed off or shut down your system. The next time you log on, Windows 8 automatically reopens those folder windows when you run the Desktop app.

---

① In any folder window, click the View tab.

② Click the top half of the Options button.

The Folder Options dialog box appears.

Note: *You can also display the Folder Options dialog box from the Start screen by pressing Windows Logo+W, typing* **folder***, and then clicking Folder Options in the search results.*

③ Click the View tab.

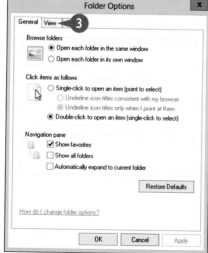

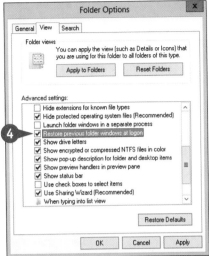

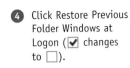

④ Click Restore Previous Folder Windows at Logon (☑ changes to ☐).

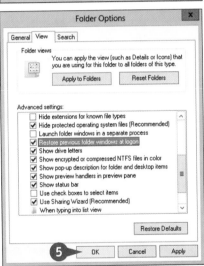

⑤ Click OK.

The next time you log on and access the Desktop app, Windows 8 restores your previous open folder windows.

Mount an ISO File

You can make it easier to work with disc image files by mounting them in File Explorer.

A *disc image* is an exact replica of the contents of an optical (CD or DVD) data disc, including the disc's file system. Each disc image is stored as an ISO (International Organization for Standardization) file that uses the .iso file extension. Many software vendors now distribute programs as ISO files, and many backup programs store their archives in the ISO format.

In previous versions of Windows, if you wanted to view or use an ISO file, you had to install a program that would burn the ISO file to an optical disc. In Windows 8, however, support for ISO files is built in to File Explorer. This means that you can view the contents of and copy data from an ISO file without third-party software. File Explorer accomplishes this by enabling you to *mount* an ISO file as a virtual optical drive on your PC.

This means you no longer need to keep copies of your optical discs. Instead, you can convert those discs to ISO files and then store them on a hard drive for easier access.

① On the Start screen, click Desktop.

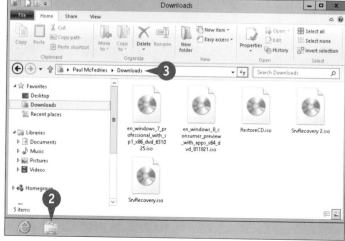

The Desktop app appears.

② Click File Explorer.

③ Open the folder that contains the ISO file you want to mount.

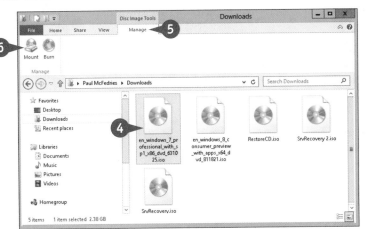

4 Click the ISO file.

5 Click the Manage tab.

6 Click Mount.

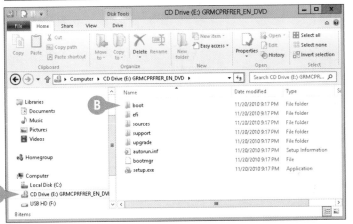

A Windows 8 creates a virtual disc drive for the ISO file.

B Windows displays the contents of the disc image.

TIPS

Try This!

If you would like to copy your own CDs and DVDs to ISO format for easier storage, backup, and transportation, Windows 8 does not come with a feature that enables you to do this. Instead, you need to download and install a third-party ISO creation program, such as Free ISO Creator, available at www.freeisocreator.com.

Reverse It!

When you no longer need to use the mounted ISO drive, you should eject it to free up the drive letter and reduce clutter in the File Explorer Folders list. To eject a mounted ISO file, use File Explorer to click the virtual disc drive. In the ribbon, click the Drive tab and then click Eject. Windows 8 unmounts the ISO file and removes the virtual disc drive.

Mount a Virtual Hard Disk

You can make it easier to work with virtual hard disk files by mounting them in File Explorer.

A *virtual hard disk* (VHD) is a disk image that contains a virtual representation of a physical hard disk, including the hard disk's partitions, file system, folders, and files. Each virtual hard disk is stored as a VHD file that uses the .vhd file extension. A virtual hard disk file is most often used as the hard disk for a virtual machine, particularly one created using the Microsoft Hyper-V virtual machine manager.

Windows 7 had limited VHD support, including the ability to boot from a VHD. In Windows 8, however, support for VHD files is built in to File Explorer. This means that you can view the contents of and copy data from a VHD file without third-party software. File Explorer accomplishes this by enabling you to *mount* a VHD as a virtual hard disk on your PC.

See the next section to learn how to create your own virtual hard disks.

---

① On the Start screen, click Desktop.

The Desktop app appears.

② Click File Explorer.

③ Open the folder that contains the VHD file you want to mount.

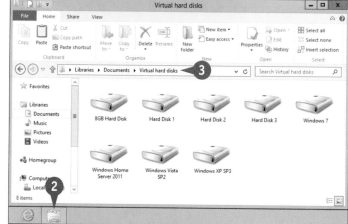

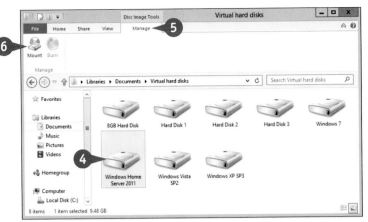

④ Click the VHD file.

⑤ Click the Manage tab.

⑥ Click Mount.

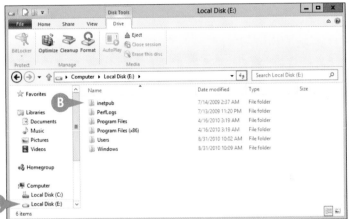

Ⓐ Windows 8 creates a virtual hard disk for the VHD.

Ⓑ Windows displays the contents of the virtual hard disk.

TIP

Reverse It!

When you no longer need to use the mounted VHD file, you should eject it to free up the drive letter and reduce clutter in the File Explorer Folders list. To eject a mounted VHD file, use File Explorer to click the virtual hard disk. In the ribbon, click the Drive tab and then click Eject. Windows 8 unmounts the VHD file and removes the virtual hard disk.

Create a Virtual Hard Disk

You can create your own virtual hard disks to get most of the benefits of having multiple hard disks without the expense of purchasing physical drives.

Having multiple hard disks attached to your PC has its advantages. For example, you can install another operating system on a separate hard disk and dual-boot between that operating system and Windows 8.

If you do not want to incur the expense of a new physical hard disk, or if your PC has no free ports

to attach a physical hard disk, you can use Windows 8 to create a virtual hard disk, which is a file that uses the VHD format. Windows 8 treats the virtual hard disk just like a regular disk, so anything you can do with a physical hard disk you can do with a VHD, including installing an operating system. You can also encrypt a VHD using BitLocker, so a VHD is an excellent way to store confidential or sensitive files.

1 On the Start screen, press Windows Logo+W.

The Settings search pane appears.

2 Type **disk**.

3 Click Create and Format Hard Disk Partitions.

The Disk Management utility appears.

4 Click Action.

5 Click Create VHD.

Disk Management displays the Create and Attach Virtual Hard Disk dialog box.

6 Click Browse.

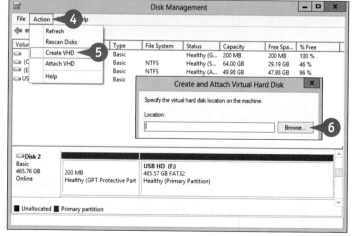

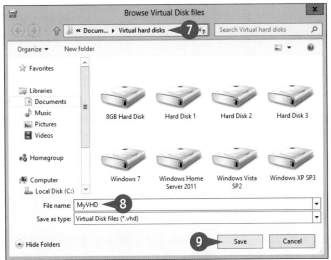

The Browse Virtual Disk Files dialog box appears.

⑦ Choose the folder you want to use to store the VHD.

⑧ Type a name for the VHD.

⑨ Click Save.

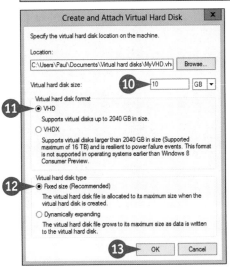

The Create and Attach Virtual Hard Disk dialog box appears.

⑩ Specify the size of the VHD, in MB, GB, or TB.

⑪ Click the Virtual Hard Disk Format you want to use (○ changes to ◉; see the tip for more information).

⑫ Choose Fixed Size (○ changes to ◉).

⑬ Click OK.

Disk Management creates the virtual hard disk.

TIPS

Did You Know?

The main differences between the VHD and VHDX virtual hard disk formats is that VHD is supported by earlier versions of Windows, but can only create disks up to 2TB; VHDX is only supported by Windows 8, but it can create disks up to 16TB. Also, VHDX is less prone to file corruption in the event of a power failure.

Important!

Before you can use the VHD, you must initialize it and create a new simple volume on the disk. Locate the new VHD in the bottom section of the Disk Management window, right-click the VHD on the left side of the window, and then click Initialize Disk. Choose MBR (○ changes to ◉) and click OK. Now follow the instructions given later in this chapter to create a new simple volume on the VHD.

Combine Multiple Drives into a Storage Pool

You can make it easier to manage multiple hard drives and work with large amounts of data by combining two or more hard dives into a single storage pool.

Multiple-terabyte (TB) hard drives are becoming commonplace. However, our data is expanding at an even faster rate as we download and rip music, TV shows, movies, and other massive media files. Nowadays, media collections that take up 10 or 20TB are not at all unusual.

Previously, the only simple way to store 10TB of data was to purchase five 2TB hard drives and split the data across the drives. This is not a

great solution because it is difficult to allocate storage efficiently and to find the file you need. Higher-end solutions such as RAID (redundant array of inexpensive disks) are complex to implement.

Windows 8 solves this problem by offering a new feature called *storage spaces*. This feature enables you to combine two or more USB, SATA, or SAS drives into a single *storage pool*, and then create a storage space — that is, a virtualized hard drive — from that pool. You can then use that space just as you would a regular hard drive.

---

① Connect the USB, SATA, or SAS drives you want to use.

② On the Start screen, press Windows Logo+W.

The Settings search pane appears.

③ Type **storage**.

④ Click Storage Spaces.

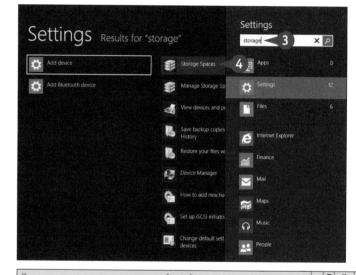

The Storage Spaces window appears.

⑤ Click Create a New Pool and Storage Space.

Windows 8 displays the User Account Control dialog box.

⑥ Click Yes.

Note: *If you are running Windows 8 using a standard account, you need to enter the credentials for an administrator account to proceed.*

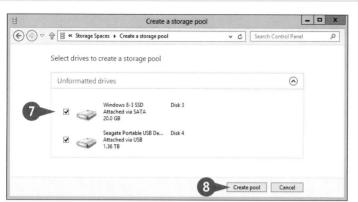

Windows 8 displays a list of drives that you can use to create the storage pool.

7 Click the check box beside each drive you want to use (☐ changes to ☑).

8 Click Create Pool.

9 Type a name for the storage pool.

10 Select a drive letter.

11 Select a resiliency type (see the first tip).

12 Type the logical size you want for the storage pool (see the second tip).

13 Click Create Storage Space.

Windows 8 pools the hard drives and creates the storage space.

TIPS

Did You Know?
Resiliency means that the storage space protects your data should a hard drive in the storage pool fail. Mirroring is the best choice here, and you can select either two-way (which creates a second copy of each file and requires at least two drives) or three-way (which creates three copies and requires at least three drives).

Did You Know?
You can specify a logical storage space size that is larger than the current physical capacity. Windows 8 will then alert you when you need to add more drives to the storage space.

More Options!
To add a drive to the storage space, follow steps 1 to 4, click Add Drives, choose the drive (☐ changes to ☑), and then click Add Drives.

Assign a Different Letter to a Disk Drive

You can assign a different drive letter to any hard disk, disk partition, CD or DVD drive, or removable drive attached to your computer.

When you installed Windows 8 on your computer, it surveyed all the disk drives on your system and assigned drive letters to each disk. For example, the drive where Windows is installed is probably drive C, your CD or DVD drive might be drive D, and if you have Flash drive or memory card slots on your PC, they were assigned letters beginning with E.

There may be times when you need or want to change the default drive letters. For example, some programs require a floppy disk drive for certain actions, and it is a rare PC that comes with a floppy drive these days. In most cases you can fool the program into thinking your system has a floppy drive by assigning drive A to a Flash drive or memory card slot.

1 On the Start screen, press Windows Logo+W.

The Settings search pane appears.

2 Type **disk**.

3 Click Create and Format Hard Disk Partitions.

The Disk Management window appears.

4 Right-click the drive you want to work with.

Note: See the Caution in the tip section before selecting a drive.

5 Click Change Drive Letter and Paths.

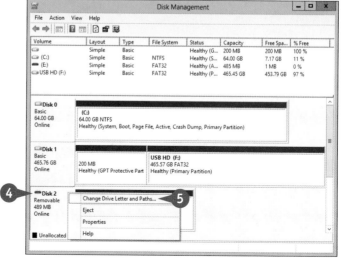

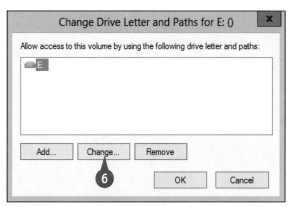

The Change Drive Letter and Paths dialog box appears.

⑥ Click Change.

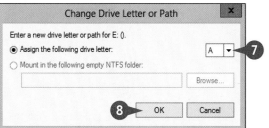

The Change Drive Letter or Path dialog box appears.

⑦ Use this list to click the drive letter you want to use.

⑧ Click OK.

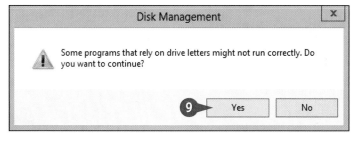

Windows 8 asks you to confirm.

⑨ Click Yes.

Windows 8 assigns the new drive letter to the disk drive.

TIPS

Caution!
Do not attempt to assign or change the drive letters associated with drive C. This drive is crucial for the operation of your PC, and modifying its drive letter could render your computer unusable.

Did You Know?
If you do not see drive A in the list of possible drive letters, it likely means that Windows 8 mistakenly believes your system has a floppy drive. To disable this "device," press Windows Logo+W, type **device**, and then click Device Manager. Open the Floppy Disk Drives branch, click Floppy Disk Drive, click Action, click Disable, and then click Yes.

Hide Disk Drive Letters

You can make the Computer folder neater-looking and less cluttered by configuring Windows 8 to not show the letters associated with each disk drive on your system.

Disk drive letters have been part of computing for decades. The letters were straightforward back when PCs had only a few disk drives, such as A for the floppy drive, C for the hard drive, and D for the CD or DVD drive.

However, in recent years the number of disk drives attached to a computer has grown quickly. Floppy drives are a distant memory, but hard drives often have multiple partitions, USB Flash drives are commonplace, many PCs come with multi-slot memory card readers, you can now mount ISO and VHD files, and all of these drives get their own letter. So it is now common for PCs to assign 10 or 15 drive letters.

Unfortunately, the more drive letters you see in the Computer window, the more cluttered the window appears, and the less meaning each letter has. In many cases, you will probably be better off if you hide the drive letters and assign meaningful names to each drive.

1. On the Start screen, click Desktop.

2. Click File Explorer.
3. Click Computer.
4. Click the View tab.
5. Click the top half of the Options button.

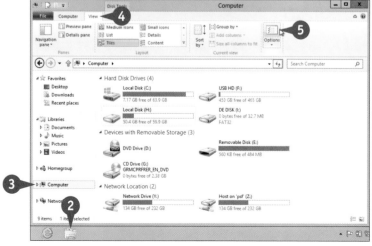

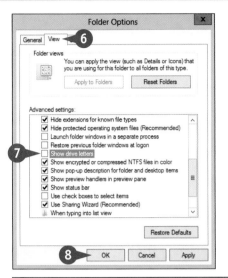

The Folder Options dialog box appears.

6 Click the View tab.

7 Click Show Drive Letters (☑ changes to ☐).

8 Click OK.

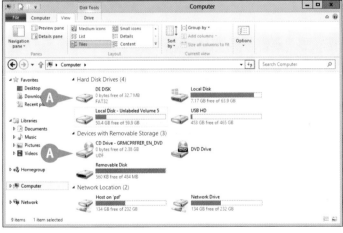

A Windows 8 no longer displays drive letters.

TIPS

Important!

Windows 8 usually provides the same "name" to similar drives. For example, removable drives such as Flash drives and memory cards are usually named Removable Disk. To help differentiate your disks when you hide drive letters, add meaningful names to your drives.

Try This!

To rename a disk drive, open the Computer window, right-click the drive you want to work with, and then click Rename. Windows 8 places a text box around the existing name. Type the new name — you can enter a maximum of 32 characters — in the text box, and then press Enter.

Split a Hard Drive into Two Partitions

You can create a separate storage area on your system by splitting your hard drive into two partitions.

In hard drive circles, a *partition* — also called a *volume* — is a subset of a hard drive that you can access and work with as a separate unit. Most hard drives consist of just a single partition that takes up the entire disk, and that partition is almost always drive C. However, it is possible to divide a single hard drive into two partitions and assign a drive letter to each — say, C and D.

Although many partition operations are better left to third-party programs such as Partition Manager (www.acronis.com) or Partition Wizard (www.partitionwizard.com), splitting a partition is something you can do using Windows 8 tools.

In this section, you learn how to divide a hard drive into two partitions. You do that by first shrinking the existing partition and then creating the new partition in the freed-up disk space.

① On the Start screen, press Windows Logo+W.

The Settings search pane appears.

② Type **disk**.

③ Click Create and Format Hard Disk Partitions.

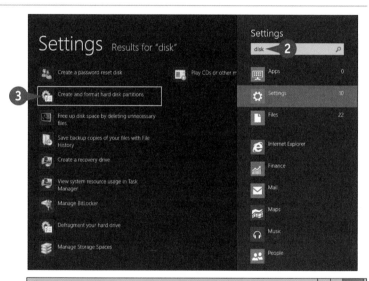

The Disk Management window appears.

④ Right-click the hard drive you want to split.

⑤ Click Shrink Volume.

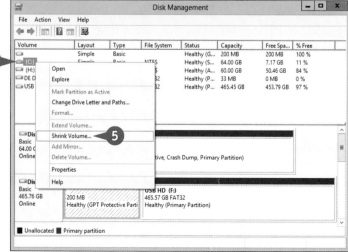

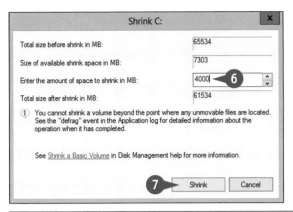

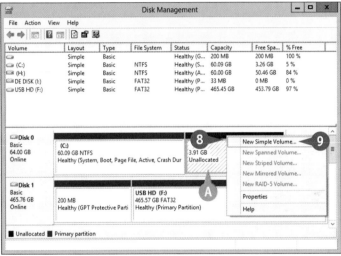

Disk Management displays the Shrink *D:* dialog box (where *D* is the drive letter of the partition).

6 Use the Enter the Amount of Space to Shrink in MB text box to type the amount by which you want the partition size reduced.

Note: This will be the approximate size of the new partition that you create later. Also see the tip section.

7 Click Shrink.

Windows 8 shrinks the partition.

A Windows 8 displays the freed space as Unallocated.

8 Right-click the unallocated space.

9 Click New Simple Volume.

TIPS

Important!

You cannot enter a shrink size that is larger than the shrink space you have at your disposal, which is given by the Size of Available Shrink Space in MB value. If you are shrinking drive C, the available shrink space will be a lot less than the available free space because Windows reserves quite a bit of space on drive C for certain system files that may grow over time.

Did You Know?

How much you shrink the partition depends on how large you want your new partition to be. For example, if you want to use the new partition to store your data, and you currently have 20GB of data, shrink the partition by 30GB to give you some extra room for new files.

continued ▶

Why would you need to split a hard disk into two partitions?

One reason you would do this is to separate your data from Windows. That is, you would create a second partition and then move your data to that partition. This is a good idea because if you ever have to reinstall Windows from scratch, you can wipe the data from drive C without having to worry about your other data, which remains intact on the other partition.

Another use for a second hard drive partition is to install a second operating system on your computer and dual-boot between Windows 8 and that operating system. In this case, you would create a second partition and then install the other operating system to that partition.

It is customary for two partitions on the same hard drive to use consecutive drive letters. However, Windows 8 probably assigned your new partition a letter other than D because D is probably taken already. To work around this problem, assign a different drive letter to the current drive D and then assign D to your new partition. See "Assign a Different Letter to a Disk Drive," earlier in this chapter.

The New Simple Volume Wizard appears.

10 Click Next.

The Specify Volume Size Wizard appears.

A Windows 8 displays the maximum partition size here.

11 Make sure that the Simple Volume Size in MB text box is set to the maximum value.

12 Click Next.

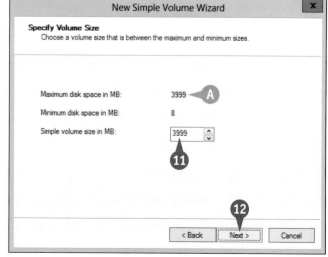

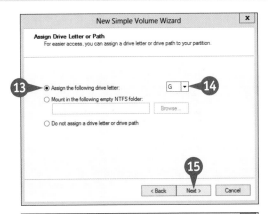

The Assign Drive Letter or Path dialog box appears.

⑬ Click Assign the Following Drive Letter (○ changes to ◉).

⑭ Use the list to select the drive letter you want to assign to the new partition.

⑮ Click Next.

The Format Partition dialog box appears.

⑯ Click the Format This Volume with the Following Settings option (○ changes to ◉).

⑰ Use the Volume Label text box to type a name for the partition.

⑱ Click Next.

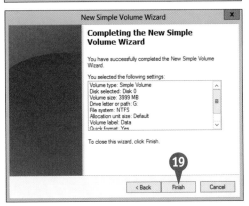

The Completing the New Simple Volume Wizard dialog box appears.

⑲ Click Finish.

Windows 8 formats the partition and assigns the drive letter.

TIP

Reverse It!
If you want to return to using a single partition, you need to first delete the extended partition. Follow steps 1 to 3 to open the Disk Management window, right-click the extended partition, and then click Delete Volume. When Windows 8 asks you to confirm, click Yes. Now right-click drive C and then click Extend Volume. In the Extend Volume Wizard, click Next, click Next, and then click Finish.

109

Enriching Your Windows 8 Media Experience

Windows 8 was designed from the ground up to offer you a rich media experience. Whether you are dealing with drawings, photos, sounds, audio CDs, downloaded music files, or DVDs, the tools built into Windows 8 enable you to play, edit, and even create media.

The downside to having a rich media environment at your fingertips is that the media tools themselves are necessarily feature-laden and complex. The basic operations are usually easy enough to master, but some of the more useful and interesting features tend to be in hard-to-find places. This chapter helps you take advantage of many of these off-the-beaten-track features by showing you how to find and use them.

For example, you discover a lot of useful image tips and tricks, including how to create custom filenames for imported images, repair image defects such as incorrect exposure and red eye, and open images for editing by default.

On the audio front, you figure out how to adjust the settings Windows Media Player uses to rip audio tracks from a CD, how to share your media library with other people on your network, how to set up an automatic playlist, and how to add sounds to Windows 8 events.

Create Custom Names for Imported Images

You can create more meaningful filenames for your imported images by configuring Photo Gallery (available from http://download.live.com) to use a custom name that you specify during each import operation.

When you import images from a device such as a digital camera, Photo Gallery launches the Import Photos and Videos tool to handle the job. By default, this tool preserves the existing filenames of the images. However, most devices supply images with cryptic filenames, such as IMG_1083 and scan001. These non-descriptive names can make it more difficult to find and work with images, particularly if you use the Details view in the Pictures folder.

To work around this problem, you can configure the Import Photos and Videos tool to apply a custom filename to your imported images. This custom filename is based on a word or short phrase that you specify during the import operation. For example, if you specify Bahamas Vacation as the import name, your imported images will be called Bahamas Vacation 001, Bahamas Vacation 002, and so on.

1 On the Start screen, click Photo Gallery.

Photo Gallery appears.

2 Click File.

3 Click Options.

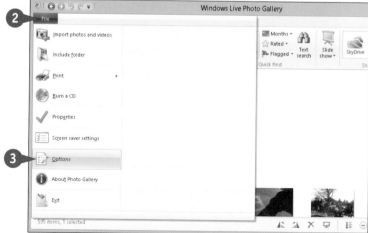

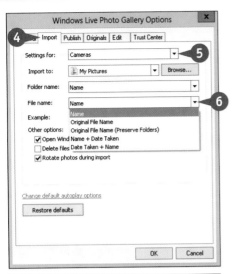

The Photo Gallery Options dialog box appears.

④ Click the Import tab.

⑤ In the Settings For list, click here and then click the type of device you want to work with.

⑥ In the File Name list, click here and then click Name.

⑦ Repeat steps 5 and 6 to apply the event tag filename to imports from other devices.

⑧ Click OK.

Photo Gallery puts the new settings into effect.

TIPS

Did You Know?

You can configure Windows 8 to always launch the Import Photos and Videos tool when you connect your digital camera. In the Import tab, click the Change Default Autoplay Options link to display the AutoPlay window. Click Choose What to Do with Each Type of Media (☐ changes to ☑). In the Pictures list, click the down arrow (▾) and then click Import Pictures and Videos Using Photo Gallery. Click Save.

More Options!

If you always clear the memory card in your digital camera after you import the images, you can have the Import Photos and Videos tool do this for you automatically. In the Import tab, click the Delete Files from Device After Importing check box (☐ changes to ☑).

Repair a Digital Photo

You can use Photo Gallery to improve the look of digital photos and other images. When you open a photo in Photo Gallery, the ribbon includes an Edit tab that offers a number of tools to repair various image attributes, including the exposure, colors, and red eye.

For the exposure, Photo Gallery can adjust both the brightness of the image and the image contrast, which is the relative difference between the lightest and darkest areas in the image.

For the color, Photo Gallery can adjust the color temperature (the relative warmth of the colors, where cooler means bluer and hotter means

redder), the tint, and the saturation (the percentage of hue in each color).

Photo Gallery also enables you to crop an image to remove unwanted subjects or to ensure that the main subject is centered in the photo.

Photo Gallery maintains a backup of the original photo, so you can always reverse any adjustments you make.

---

1. In Photo Gallery, double-click the photo you want to repair.

Photo Gallery opens the photo.

2. Click the Edit tab.

3. Click Fine Tune.

Ⓐ Photo Gallery displays the Fine Tune tools.

4. To change the exposure, click Adjust Exposure and then drag the displayed sliders.

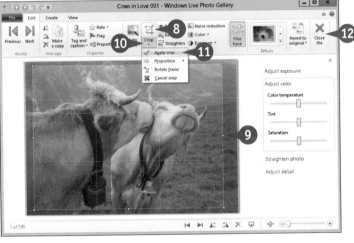

5 To change the color, click Adjust Color and then drag the Color Temperature, Tint, and Saturation sliders.

6 To straighten a photo, click Straighten Photo and then drag the slider.

Ⓑ You can click Auto Adjust to have Photo Gallery make the exposure, color, and straighten adjustments for you.

7 To remove red eye from a photo, click Red Eye and drag a rectangle around each red eye.

8 To crop the picture, click the top half of the Crop button.

9 Drag the handles to set the new size of the image.

10 Click the bottom half of the Crop button.

11 Click Apply Crop.

12 When you are done, click Close File, and Photo Gallery applies the repairs.

TIPS

More Options!

When you crop an image, Photo Gallery assumes you want the cropped version to have the same relative height and width of the original. If you do not want this, click the bottom half of the Crop button, click Proportion, and then click Custom. If you are cropping for a photo printout, click one of the standard sizes, such as 5 x 7, instead.

Reverse It!

Photo Gallery always keeps a backup copy of the original image, just in case. To undo all your changes and get the original image back, double-click the image and then click the Edit tab. Click the top half of the Revert to Original button (or press Ctrl+R). When Photo Gallery asks you to confirm, click Revert.

115

Open Images in Photo Gallery by Default

You can make it easier to work with your image files by configuring Windows 8 to automatically open them in the Photo Gallery application.

Photo Gallery is an excellent photo application that enables you to fix exposure and color problems, crop and straighten photos, convert multiple photos to a single panoramic scene, publish images to Facebook and Flickr, order prints, and much more.

Unfortunately, when you double-click a photo, Windows by default opens that file in Photos, a Windows 8 app that offers very few features. If you find that you always open your images in Photo Gallery, you can configure Windows to make that application the default for image file types. That way, you can open any image in Photo Gallery by double-clicking it.

① On the Start screen, press Windows Logo+W.

The Settings search pane appears.

② Type **default**.

③ Click Set Your Default Programs.

The Set Default Programs window appears.

④ In the Programs list, click Photo Gallery.

⑤ Click Choose Defaults for this Program.

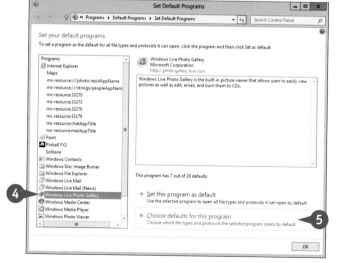

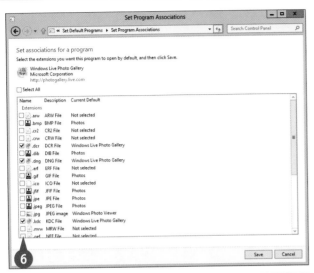

The Set Program Associations window appears.

⑥ Click the check box beside each image type you want to open in Photo Gallery (☐ changes to ☑).

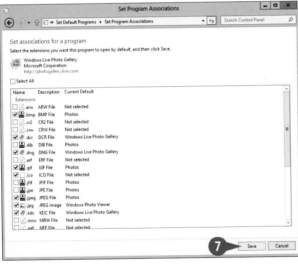

⑦ Click Save.

Windows 8 associates the selected file types with Photo Gallery.

Open an Image Type for Editing by Default

You can configure Windows 8 to always open an image file type in a graphics program for editing when you double-click the file.

For most document types, when you double-click a file, the file opens in an appropriate program for editing. For example, if you double-click a text document, Windows 8 opens the file in the Notepad text-editing program. Similarly, if you double-click a Rich Text Format document, the file opens in WordPad or Word depending on your computer's settings.

Unfortunately, Windows 8 is inconsistent when it comes to graphics files. For example, if you

double-click a bitmap image, the file does not open in the Paint graphics program. Instead, Windows 8 loads the file into the Photos app, which only allows you to view the file; you cannot edit the image. This choice is not only inconsistent, but also frustrating because now you must close the Photos app and open the file in Paint.

Fortunately, you can fix the problem by forcing Windows 8 to open an image file type in Paint or some other graphics program when you double-click the file.

① On the Start screen, type **default**.

② Click Default Programs.

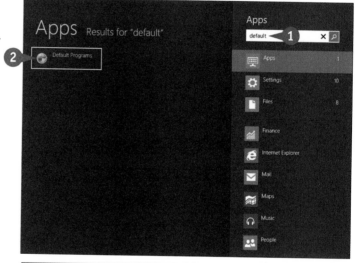

The Default Programs window appears.

③ Click Associate a File Type or Protocol with a Program.

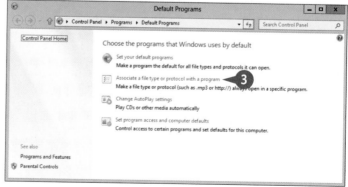

118

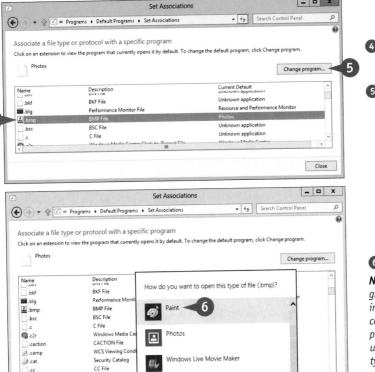

The Set Associations window appears.

④ Click the image file type you want to work with.

⑤ Click Change Program.

Windows 8 displays a list of programs that are compatible with the image file type.

⑥ Click Paint.

Note: If you have other graphics programs installed on your computer, click the program you prefer to use for editing this file type.

⑦ Click Close.

When you now double-click any of the image file types you selected in step 4, the file opens for editing in the program you selected in step 6.

TIPS

Preview It!
Just because you associated an image file type with a different application, it does not mean you can no longer use that file type with any other application. To open an image of that file type using another application, right-click the image, click Open With, and then click the program you want to use (such as Photos or Photo Gallery).

More Options!
What happens if you have a third-party graphics program that does not appear in the list of programs that are compatible with the image file type? Right-click an image of that file type, click Open With, and then click Choose Default Program. In the list, click See All. If you still do not see the program, click Look for an App on this PC. Use the new Open With dialog box to locate the graphics program. Click the program and then click Open.

Compress Your Image Files

You can compress one or more of your large image files into a smaller format, either to save space or to upload the files to a website.

Image files are often quite large. Complex bitmap images and photo-quality images from a digital camera or scanner run to several megabytes or more. A large collection of such files can easily consume gigabytes of hard drive space. If you are running low on hard drive space, but you do not want to delete any of your

image files, compressing those files into smaller versions can help.

Similarly, you may need to upload one or more of your image files to a website. You not only have to compress web images so that users with slow connections can load them in a reasonable time, but you must also convert the images to a format that all web browsers can work with.

In this section, you learn a trick that enables you to compress images and convert them to the web-friendly JPEG format.

1. Search for or open the folder that contains the images you want to compress.

2. Select the images.

A. For comparison purposes later on, note the total size of the selected images.

3. Click the Share tab.

4. Click Email.

   The Attach Files dialog box appears.

5. Use the Picture Size list to select the picture size you prefer.

6. Click Attach.

   An e-mail message window opens with the images shown as a photo album.

7. Click an image.

8. Click the Format tab.

9. Click Attach Photos to this Email Message.

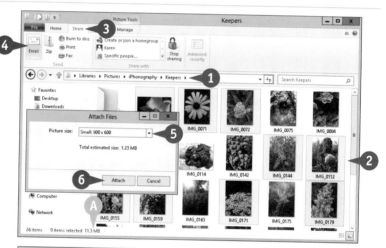

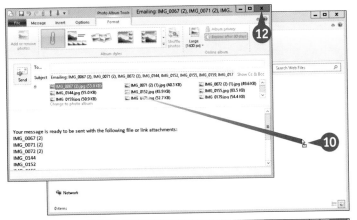

Mail converts the files to attachments.

⑩ Click and drag an attachment and drop it inside a folder.

⑪ Repeat step 10 for each attached file.

⑫ Click Close.

Mail asks if you want to save the message.

⑬ Click No (not shown).

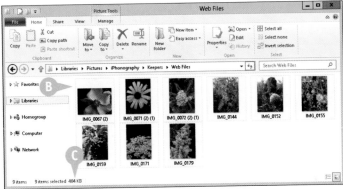

Ⓑ The images appear in the folder.

Ⓒ The images are now compressed and take up less space on your hard drive.

Note: If you still have the original images, either delete them or archive them to a removable drive.

TIPS

More Options!

If your goal is to save hard drive space, you can place infrequently used images in a compressed folder. This is a special folder that shrinks the images as much as possible. When you want to work with one of the original files, you can extract it from the compressed folder at any time. To create the compressed folder, select the images you want to compress, right-click one of the selected images, and then click Send To, Compressed (Zipped) Folder. Delete the original images after Windows 8 creates the compressed folder.

Check It Out!

For maximum control over compressing image files, you can use a third-party graphics program, such as Paint Shop Pro (available from www.corel.com) or the free programs IrfanView (www.irfanview.com) or Easy Thumbnails (www.notetab.com).

121

Play Music Files in Windows Media Player by Default

You can get more out of your digital music files by configuring Windows 8 to automatically open them in the Windows Media Player program.

Windows Media Player is a first-rate program that enables you to perform a number of high-level tasks related to music files. For example, you can organize your music into playlists, as described in the next section. You can also use Windows Media Player to rip tracks from audio CDs, share your music library with other people on your network, and access libraries that others have shared.

Unfortunately, when you double-click a music file, Windows by default opens that file in Music, a Windows 8 app that offers only a very limited number of features. If you find that you always open your music files in Windows Media Player, you can configure Windows to make that application the default for music file types. That way, you can open any music file in Windows Media Player by double-clicking it.

① On the Start screen, press Windows Logo+W.

The Settings search pane appears.

② Type **default**.

③ Click Set Your Default Programs.

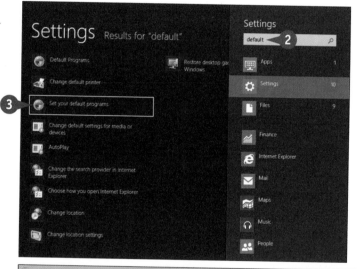

The Set Default Programs window appears.

④ In the Programs list, click Windows Media Player.

⑤ Click Choose Defaults for this Program.

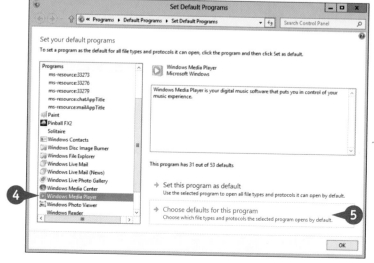

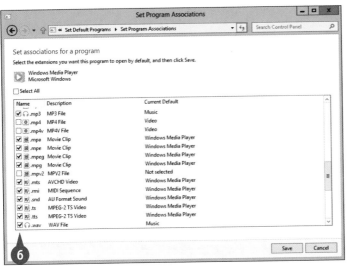

The Set Program Associations window appears.

⑥ Click the check box beside each image type you want to open in Windows Media Player (☐ changes to ☑).

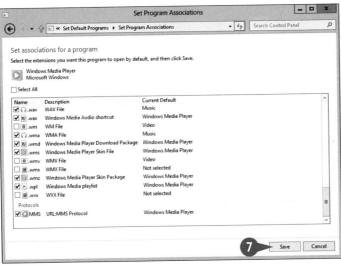

⑦ Click Save.

Windows 8 associates the selected file types with Windows Media Player.

Did You Know?

The most common music file types that you should associate with Windows Media Player are AAC File (.aac), AIF File (.aif), AIFF File (.aiff), MP3 File (.mp3), WAV File (.wav), and WMA File (.wma).

Add It Automatically!

If you know you want to use Windows Media Player for every music (and video) file type, you can quickly set the program as the default for those types. Follow steps 1 to 3 to open the Set Default Programs window and select Windows Media Player. Then click Set this Program as Default.

123

Create an Automatic Playlist

You can create a playlist that Windows Media Player maintains automatically based on the criteria you specify.

You normally create a playlist by clicking and dragging music files to the playlist. However, you can also create a playlist based on the properties that Windows Media Player maintains for each file. These properties include Album Artist, Genre, Composer, and Rating, to name just a few. So, for example, you could create a playlist that includes every music file where the Genre property equals Folk.

You create a property-based playlist by specifying the playlist *criteria*, which consist of three factors: the property, the property value, and an operator that relates the two. The most common operators are Is, Is Not, and Contains. For the folk music example, the criteria would be the following: Genre Is Folk.

The best part about property-based playlists is that they are automatic. This means that after you set up the playlist, Windows Media Player automatically populates the playlist with all the music files that meet your criteria.

① On the Start screen, type **media** and then click Windows Media Player.

② Click the arrow beside Create Playlist.

③ Click Create Auto Playlist.

The New Auto Playlist dialog box appears.

④ Type a name for the playlist.

⑤ Click here to display the menu of properties.

⑥ Click a property.

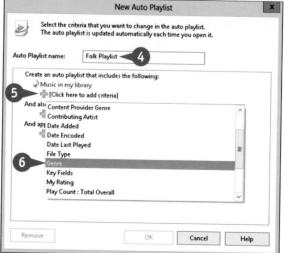

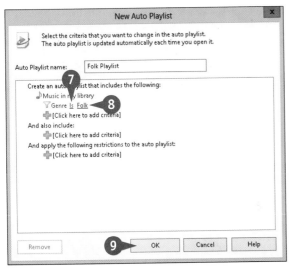

⑦ Click here to choose an operator.

⑧ Click here and then click the criteria you want to use.

⑨ Click OK.

Ⓐ Windows Media Player adds your playlist to Playlists.

Ⓑ Windows Media Player populates the playlist based on your criteria.

TIPS

More Options!

You can place restrictions on your automatic playlists so that they do not become too large. Open the Playlists branch, right-click your automatic playlist, and then click Edit to display the Edit Auto Playlist dialog box. Pull down the list named And Apply the Following Restrictions to the Auto Playlist, and then click Limit Number of Items, Limit Total Duration To, or Limit Total Size To. Fill in the limit, and then click OK.

Remove It!

If you no longer need your automatic playlist, you should delete it so that Windows Media Player does not keep updating it and to reduce clutter in the Playlists branch. Right-click the playlist and then click Delete. In the confirmation dialog box that appears, click Delete from Library and My Computer, and then click OK.

Adjust Rip Settings

Windows Media Player gives you a lot of control over the copying — or *ripping* — of tracks from an audio CD by enabling you to select a format and a bit rate.

The *format* is the audio file type you want to use to store the ripped tracks on your computer. You have five choices:

The Windows Media Audio format compresses audio by removing extraneous sounds not normally detected by the human ear.

The Windows Media Audio (variable bit rate) format changes the compression depending on the audio data: If the data is more complex, it uses less compression to keep the quality high.

The Windows Media Audio Lossless format does not compress the audio tracks.

The MP3 format also compresses the audio files to make them smaller, but MP3s are generally about twice the size of WMA files.

The WAV format is an uncompressed audio file format compatible with all versions of Windows.

The *bit rate* determines the quality of the rip and is measured in kilobits per second (Kbps). The higher the bit rate, the better the quality, but the more hard drive space each track uses.

Use the Rip Settings Menu

1 Insert an audio CD.

2 In Windows Media Player, click the audio CD.

3 Click Rip Settings.

4 Click Format.

Windows Media Player displays the available audio file formats.

5 Click the format you want to use.

6 Click Rip Settings.

7 Click Audio Quality.

Windows Media Player displays the available bit rates.

Note: *The available bit rates depend on the audio file format you chose in step 5. Note that some formats use a fixed bit rate that you cannot change.*

8 Click the bit rate you want to use.

Windows Media Player uses the new settings the next time you rip tracks from an audio CD.

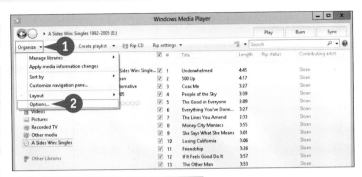

Use the Options Dialog Box

1 Click Organize.

2 Click Options.

The Options dialog box appears.

3 Click the Rip Music tab.

4 Use the Format list to click the format you want to use.

5 Click the Audio Quality slider to select the bit rate you want to use.

6 Click OK.

Windows Media Player uses the new settings the next time you rip tracks from an audio CD.

TIP

Did You Know?
The bit rate determines the size of each ripped track. There are 8 bits in a byte, 1,024 bytes in a kilobyte, and 1,024 kilobytes in a megabyte. The following table lists the bit rates for the Windows Media Audio format and how much drive space it uses. Note that although the Audio Quality slider says "per CD," the values it displays are per hour):

Bit Rates and Drive Space for the WMA Format		
Bit Rate (Kbps)	**KB/Minute**	**MB/Hour**
48	360	22
64	480	28
96	720	42
128	960	56
160	1,200	69
192	1,440	86

Customize the Data Displayed by Windows Media Player

You can see just the information you want for every media file by customizing the Windows Media Player view to show the specific media details you prefer.

Windows Media Player keeps track of a great deal of information for all your media files. For music files, Windows Media Player keeps track of standard properties, such as the album title, artist, and the track names and lengths. However, Windows Media Player also stores more detailed information, such as the genre, release date, bit rate, file format, and size.

For videos, Windows Media Player stores standard properties, such as the title, length, and size,

but also in some cases more detailed information, such as number of frames per second and the bit rate for both the video and audio tracks. For some commercial videos, you can also view the director, actors, and studio.

These properties are called *metadata* because they are all data that describe the media. You can customize any of the Windows Media Player folders to display the Details view, which shows the metadata. Further, you can customize the specific metadata columns that Windows Media Player displays in each view.

Switch to Details View

① In Windows Media Player, click here to open the View Options menu.

② Click Details.

Windows Media Player switches to Details view.

Customize Columns

① Click Organize.

② Click Layout.

③ Click Choose Columns.

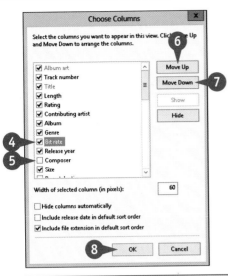

The Choose Columns dialog box appears.

④ Click the deactivated check boxes of the columns you want to view (☐ changes to ☑).

⑤ Click to uncheck the activated check boxes of the columns you do not want to view (☑ changes to ☐).

⑥ To move the selected column to the left in Details view, click Move Up.

⑦ To move the selected column to the right in Details view, click Move Down.

⑧ Click OK.

Ⓐ Windows Media Player updates the view to display the columns you selected.

More Options!
You can see more columns in Details view if you reduce the width of each column so that it is just wide enough to display its data. The easiest way to do this is to position the mouse pointer over the right edge of the column's header — ↳ changes to ↔ — and then double-click.

More Options!
You can change the order of the Details view columns without displaying the Choose Columns dialog box. Simply use your mouse to click and drag the column header to the left or right and then drop it in the new position.

129

Share Your Media Library with Others

You can listen to the songs and view the photos and videos in your Windows Media Player library on another device by sharing your library over a wired or wireless network.

If you have spent a great deal of time ripping audio CDs, downloading music files, adding other media to your library, and organizing the library, you probably do not want to repeat all that work on another computer. If you have a wired or wireless network, however, you can take advantage of the library work you have done on one computer by sharing — or *streaming* — that library over the network. This enables any other computer using Windows 8 to include your media in that machine's Windows Media Player library. This also applies to other user accounts on your computer. Those users can log on and then access your shared library.

Your shared library is also available to other media devices on the network, such as an Xbox 360 or a networked digital media receiver.

Turn On Media Streaming

1. In Windows Media Player, click Stream.

2. Click Turn On Media Streaming.

The Media Streaming Options window appears.

3. Click Turn On Media Streaming.

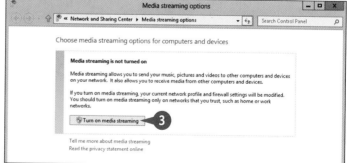

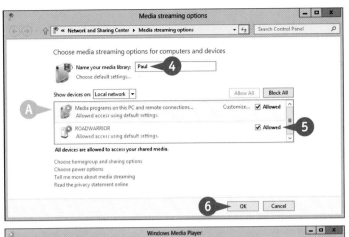

Windows Media Player turns on media streaming and displays the streaming options.

④ Type a name for your media library.

Ⓐ Windows Media Player displays a list of the devices that can access your media library.

⑤ For each device, click Allowed (☐ changes to ☑) if you want the device to access your media library.

⑥ Click OK.

Access a Shared Media Library

① In the Windows Media Player navigation pane, click the name of the library you want to access.

② Double-click the type of media you want to play.

Note: *Although other computers can usually see the shared library within a few seconds, the media in the shared library may take several minutes to appear.*

More Options!
To restrict the media you share, click Stream and then click More Streaming Options. To set restrictions for all devices, click Choose Default Settings; otherwise, click a device and then click Customize. Under Star Rating, click Only (◯ changes to ◉) and then click a rating. Under Choose Parental Ratings, click Only (◯ changes to ◉), and then click the check boxes of the ratings you do not want to share (☑ changes to ☐).

More Options!
You can also allow network devices to control your local Windows Media Player, which enables those devices to add music and other media to your library. To set this up, click Stream and then click Allow Remote Control of My Player. In the Allow Remote Control dialog box, click Allow Remote Control on This Network.

You can customize various aspects of the Windows Media Player navigation pane to suit the way you use Windows Media Player.

The navigation pane on the left side of the Windows Media Player window gives you a quick way to switch from one Windows Media Player library to another. However, the navigation pane is also an easy way to use media properties to get different views of your media.

For example, by default the Music section of the navigation pane includes three subsections:

Artist, Album, and Genre. When you click one of these subsections, you see your music organized by the corresponding property values (artist name, album title, or genre).

You can customize the navigation to show other music properties, such as Rating and Year, as well as properties for the other sections: Videos, Pictures, and Recorded TV.

Windows Media Player also enables you to customize the navigation pane to show all your playlists and to hide the Other Media section.

① Click Organize.

② Click Customize Navigation Pane.

The Customize Navigation Pane dialog box appears.

③ If you want to see all your playlists in the Playlists section, click All (☐ changes to ✔).

④ Click the check box for each category you want to include in the Music section (☐ changes to ✔).

⑤ Click the check box for each category you want to include in the Videos section (☐ changes to ✔).

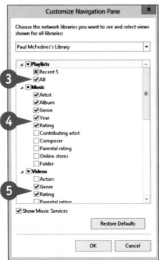

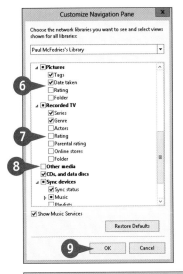

⑥ Click the check box for each category you want to include in the Pictures section (☐ changes to ☑).

⑦ Click the check box for each category you want to include in the Recorded TV section (☐ changes to ☑).

⑧ Click Other Media to hide this section (☑ changes to ☐).

⑨ Click OK.

Ⓐ Windows Media Player applies the new settings to the navigation pane.

⑩ Click and drag the divider to change the width of the navigation pane as needed.

133

Add Sounds to Windows 8 Events

You can associate sound files with specific Windows 8 occurrences, such as minimizing a window or starting a program. This not only adds some aural variety to your system, but it can also help novice users of your computer follow and understand what is happening on the screen.

In Windows 8, a *program event* is an action taken by a program or by Windows 8 itself in response to something. For example, if you click a window's Minimize button, the window minimizes to the taskbar. Similarly, if you click an item in a program's menu bar, the menu drops down. Other events, such as an error

message, a low notebook battery alarm, or a notification of the arrival of a new e-mail message, are generated internally by a program or by Windows 8.

Windows 8 has certain sounds associated with all of these events and many others. Some of these sounds, such as the music you hear when Windows 8 starts up, are purely decorative "ear candy." Other sounds, such as the sharp tone that sounds when an error message appears, are more useful. Whether your goal is aural decoration or usefulness, you can augment or change the existing Windows 8 sounds.

1 On the Start screen, press Windows Logo+W.

2 Type **system sounds**.

3 Click Change System Sounds.

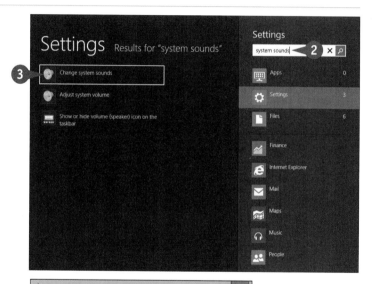

The Sound dialog box appears with the Sounds tab displayed.

4 Click the Windows 8 event you want to work with.

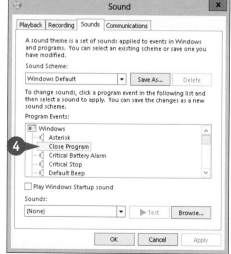

134

5 Click here and then click the sound you want to associate with the event.

A If the sound you want does not appear in the Sounds list, click Browse and use the Browse for New Sound dialog box to choose the sound file you want.

6 Click Test to listen to the sound.

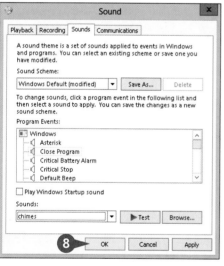

7 Repeat steps 4 to 6 to assign sounds to other Windows 8 events.

8 Click OK.

In this example, the next time you close a program, Windows plays a chimes sound.

TIPS

More Options!

You can save your selected sounds as a *sound scheme*, a collection of sound files associated with Windows 8 events. In the Sounds tab of the Sound dialog box, after you have made your sound selections, click Save As, type a name for the sound scheme, and then click OK.

Remove It!

If you tire of your sound scheme and prefer to return Windows 8 to its original sound settings, follow steps 1 to 3 to open the Sound dialog box. Click ⬛ in the Sound Scheme list and then click Windows Default. If you prefer no sounds at all, click No Sounds. Click OK.

Chapter

6

Maximizing Windows 8 Performance

Whether you use Windows 8 at work or at home, you probably want to spend your computer time creating documents, sending and receiving e-mail, browsing the web, playing games, and doing other useful and fun activities. You probably do *not* want to spend your time wrestling with Windows 8 or waiting for it to finish its tasks.

Using a few simple techniques, you can make working with Windows 8 faster and more convenient. For example, Windows 8 offers many keyboard shortcuts that can save you a great deal of time compared to using your mouse. Similarly, instead of wasting time logging on to Windows 8, you can configure the system to log you on automatically.

Also, you can work with a few settings to ensure Windows 8 is working quickly and efficiently. For example, you can locate your files faster by tweaking the Windows search engine.

Sometimes getting the most out of Windows 8 is a simple matter of taking care of the little details. For example, you can make Windows 8 more efficient by configuring it to automatically move the mouse pointer to the default button in a dialog box, and to not prompt you for confirmation when you delete a file.

This chapter introduces you to these and many other techniques for maximizing your Windows 8 productivity.

Learn Windows 8 Keyboard Shortcuts

Windows 8 was made with the mouse in mind, so most day-to-day tasks are designed to be performed using the standard mouse moves. However, this does not mean your keyboard should be ignored when you are not typing.

Windows 8 is loaded with keyboard shortcuts and techniques that can be used as replacements for mouse clicks and drags. These shortcuts are often a faster way to work because you do not have to move your hand from the keyboard to the mouse and back. Also, the Windows 8 keyboard techniques are useful to know just in case you have problems with your mouse and must rely on the keyboard to get your work done.

Windows Logo Shortcut Keys	
Press	**To do this**
Windows Logo	Switch between the Start screen and the most recent Windows 8 app
Windows Logo+B	Switch to the desktop and activates the taskbar's Show Hidden Icons arrow
Windows Logo+C	Display the Charms menu
Windows Logo+D	Switch to the Desktop app
Windows Logo+E	Run File Explorer
Windows Logo+F	Display the Files search pane
Windows Logo+H	Display the Share pane
Windows Logo+I	Display the Settings pane
Windows Logo+K	Display the Devices pane
Windows Logo+L	Lock your computer
Windows Logo+M	Switch to the desktop and minimize all windows
Windows Logo+O	Turn the tablet orientation lock on and off
Windows Logo+P	Switch to a second display
Windows Logo+Q	Display the Apps search pane
Windows Logo+R	Open the Run dialog box
Windows Logo+T	Switch to the desktop and cycle through the taskbar icons
Windows Logo+U	Open the Ease of Access Center
Windows Logo+W	Display the Settings search pane
Windows Logo+X	Display a menu of Windows tools and utilities
Windows Logo+Z	Display the application bar in a Windows 8 app
Windows Logo+=	Open Magnifier and zoom in
Windows Logo+-	Zoom out (if already zoomed in using Magnifier)
Windows Logo+,	Temporarily display the desktop
Windows Logo+Enter	Open Narrator
Windows Logo+PgUp	Move the current Windows 8 app to the left-hand monitor
Windows Logo+PgDn	Move the current Windows 8 app to the right-hand monitor
Windows Logo+PrtSc	Capture the current screen and save it to the Pictures folder
Windows Logo+Tab	Switch between running Windows 8 apps

General Windows Shortcut Keys

Press	To do this
Ctrl+Alt+Delete	Display the Windows Security screen
Ctrl+-	Zoom out of the Start screen
Ctrl+=	Zoom in to the Start screen

Shortcut Keys for Working with Program Windows

Press	To do this
Alt	Activate or deactivate a desktop program's menu bar
Alt+Esc	Cycle through the open desktop program windows
Alt+F4	Close the active program window
Alt+Spacebar	Display the system menu for the active program window
Alt+Tab	Cycle through icons for running programs (Windows 8 and desktop)
F1	Display context-sensitive Help

Shortcut Keys for Working with Documents

Press	To do this
Alt+-	Display the system menu for the active document window
Ctrl+F4	Close the active document window
Ctrl+F6	Cycle through the open documents within an application
Ctrl+N	Create a new document
Ctrl+O	Display the Open dialog box
Ctrl+P	Display the Print dialog box
Ctrl+S	Save the current file; if the file is new, display the Save As dialog box

Shortcut Keys for Working with Data

Press	To do this
Backspace	Delete the character to the left of the insertion point
Ctrl+C	Copy the selected data to memory
Ctrl+F	Display the Find dialog box
Ctrl+H	Display the Replace dialog box
Ctrl+X	Cut the selected data to memory
Ctrl+V	Paste the most recently cut or copied data from memory
Ctrl+Z	Undo the most recent action
Delete	Delete the selected data
F3	Repeat the most recent Find operation

139

Start Faster by Logging On Automatically

You can configure your Windows 8 system to start faster by bypassing the Welcome screen and logging on your user account automatically.

When you start your computer, your system first tests various components during the *power on self test* (POST) routine, and then Windows 8 loads its components into memory. You eventually end up at the lock screen, where you must press Enter, click your user icon (if your system has multiple user accounts), and then type your account password. Only then does Windows 8 finish loading and display the desktop.

Logging on is not an onerous task, but it does slow down the startup. This is particularly true if you want to power on your computer and then go perform some other task while the system boots, because you must return to the PC to perform the logon.

To save the time it takes to log on, and to enable Windows to completely load the system without requiring any input from you, you can configure Windows 8 to automatically log on your user account.

---

① On the Start screen, type **run**.

② Click Run.

The Run dialog box appears.

Note: You can also display the Run dialog box by pressing Windows Logo+R.

③ Type **control userpasswords2**.

④ Click OK.

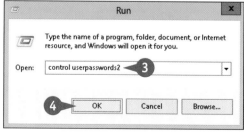

The User Accounts dialog box appears.

⑤ Click the user account you want to log on automatically.

⑥ Click Users Must Enter a User Name and Password to Use This Computer (☑ changes to ☐).

⑦ Click OK.

The Automatically Sign In dialog box appears.

⑧ Type the account's password.

⑨ Type the account's password again.

⑩ Click OK.

The next time you start your computer, Windows 8 automatically logs on your user account.

TIPS

Caution!

Many forms of Windows 8 security — including User Account Control, file encryption, local file security, and network file sharing — assume that the logged-on user is a trusted user who has provided the proper logon credentials to access the system. This section's technique bypasses that logon, so use it only if no other person has physical access to your computer.

Try This!

If you have other accounts on your system, you can still log on one of them. Wait until your account logs on automatically and you see the Start screen. Click your user account tile, and then click either another user's account (to keep your account logged on), or Sign Out (to log off your account). Either way, you end up at the login screen where you can log on the other account.

Automatically Move the Mouse to the Default Button

You can negotiate many dialog boxes much more quickly by customizing Windows 8 to automatically move the mouse pointer over the default dialog box button.

Most dialog boxes define a *default button* as the button that dismisses the dialog box and puts the dialog box settings into effect. The most common default dialog box button is the OK button.

Windows 8 makes it easy for you to find the default button by making the button glow while the dialog box is open. That is, the button's blue color gradually fades in and out.

Many dialog boxes do nothing more than provide you with information or a warning. In most of these cases, the only thing you need to do with the dialog box is click the default button. You can get past such dialog boxes much more quickly if you configure Windows 8 to use the Snap To feature, which automatically moves the mouse pointer over the default button, because then all you have to do is click to dismiss the dialog box. If the dialog box requires more complex input from you, you still save time because the mouse pointer is already inside the dialog box.

---

1 On the Start screen, type **control**.

2 Click Control Panel.

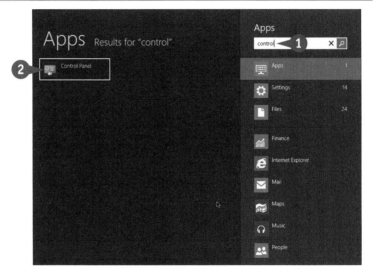

The Control Panel window appears.

3 Click Hardware and Sound.

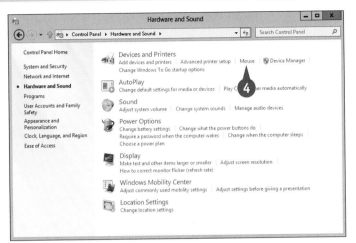

The Hardware and Sound window appears.

④ Click Mouse.

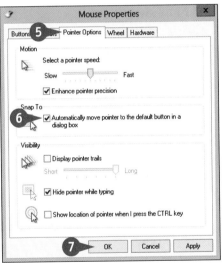

The Mouse Properties dialog box appears.

⑤ Click the Pointer Options tab.

⑥ Click the Automatically Move Pointer to the Default Button in a Dialog Box check box (☐ changes to ☑).

⑦ Click OK.

Windows 8 automatically moves the mouse pointer to the default button each time you open a dialog box.

TIPS

Caution!
When the Snap To feature is activated, it is easy to get into the habit of quickly clicking whenever a notification dialog box appears. However, if you click too quickly, you may miss the message in the dialog box, which could be important. Remember to read all dialog box messages before clicking the default button.

More Options!
If you have excellent mouse control, another option that can save time in the long run is to increase the pointer speed, which enables you to get from one part of the screen to another much more quickly. Follow steps 1 to 5 to display the Pointer Options tab, click and drag the Select a Pointer Speed slider towards Fast, and then click OK.

143

Open Files Faster by Using Metadata Searches

You can take advantage of the many file properties supported by Windows 8 to search for files based on the author, keywords, and other data.

In Windows 8, you can perform sophisticated searches by using a number of different properties. These file properties are called *metadata* because they are data that describe the data on your system — that is, your documents. To add metadata, right-click a document, click Properties, and then use the Details tab.

For example, the Authors property specifies the name of the person (or people) who created a

document. Similarly, the Tags property lists one or more words or phrases that describe the contents of a document.

Some metadata is added to files automatically. For example, photo metadata properties include the Dimensions, Camera Model, and Exposure Time. Similarly, for music files, you can search on the Genre name, Album title, Artist name, and more.

You can create advanced searches that look in these and other properties for the file or files you seek.

---

① Open the folder you want to search in.

Note: *If you want to search your entire computer, press Windows Logo+F to open the Files search pane.*

② Click inside the Search box.

Ⓐ Windows 8 displays the Search tab.

③ Click a property.

④ Click a value.

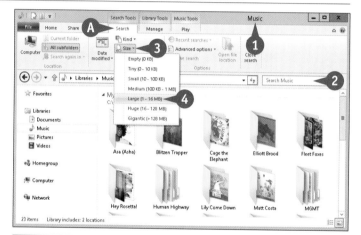

Ⓑ Windows 8 adds the search criteria to the Search box.

Ⓒ Windows 8 displays the files that match the property value.

⑤ Click Other Properties.

⑥ Click a property.

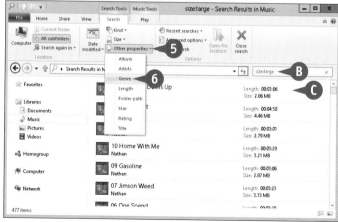

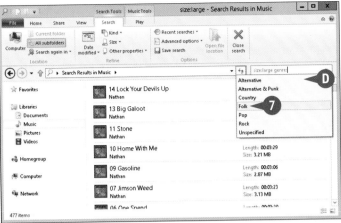

ⓓ Windows 8 displays the available property values.

❼ Click the property value you want to use in your search.

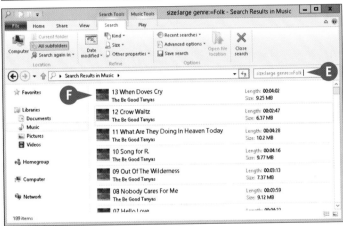

ⓔ Windows 8 adds the search criteria to the Search box.

ⓕ Windows 8 displays the files that match the property value.

❽ Repeat steps 3 to 7 to add more metadata to your search criteria.

Windows 8 displays the files that match all of your values.

TIPS

More Options!

By default, Windows 8 matches only those files that satisfy all of the criteria you add to the Search box. However, there may be times when you are looking for files that match one criterion or another. For example, you might want to find music where the Genre property is Folk or Fiddle. To perform such a search, insert the word OR between the criteria, as in this example:

Genre:=Folk OR Genre:=Fiddle

More Options!

By default, Windows 8 looks for files where the property equals the value you specify. To match files where the property does not equal the value, add the not equals sign (<>) after the colon, as in this example:

Year:2000 Genre:<> Rock

Search Files Faster by Adding a Folder to the Index

You can add folders to the Windows Search engine's index, which makes your file searches in those folders run noticeably faster.

Having a lot of data is certainly not a bad thing, but *finding* the file you want among all that data can be frustrating. Fortunately, the Windows 8 Search feature can help by enabling you to search for files based on name, content, size, and more.

This works well if what you are looking for is in your main user account folder or one of its file libraries (such as the Documents, Pictures, or

Music library). This is because Windows 8 automatically *indexes* those folders, which means it keeps a detailed record of the contents of all your files. Using this index, the Search feature can find files up to a hundred times faster than without an index.

However, if you have files in a different location, Windows 8 does not index them, so searching those files is very time-consuming. You can dramatically speed up the searching of those files by adding their location to the Search index.

---

① On the Start screen, press Windows Logo+W.

The Settings search pane appears.

② Type **index**.

③ Click Indexing Options.

The Indexing Options dialog box appears.

④ Click Modify.

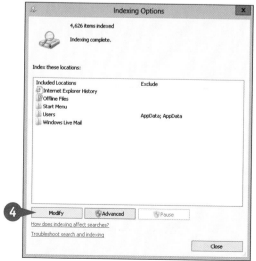

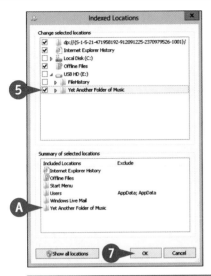

The Indexed Locations dialog box appears.

⑤ Click the check box beside the folder you want to include in the index (☐ changes to ☑).

Ⓐ The folder appears in the list of included locations.

⑥ Repeat step 5 to add other folders to the index.

⑦ Click OK.

⑧ Click Close.

Windows 8 includes the folder in the index and begins rebuilding the index.

TIPS

Did You Know?

If Windows 8 takes a long time to search or cannot find your files, you may need to rebuild the index. Follow steps 1 to 3 to display the Indexing Options dialog box. Click Advanced to display the Advanced Options dialog box, and then click Rebuild.

Caution!

The catalog created by the Indexing Service can use up hundreds of megabytes of hard drive space. To move the catalog to a hard drive with more space, follow steps 1 to 3 to display the Indexing Options dialog box. Click Advanced to display the Advanced Options dialog box. Click Select New, select a new location, and then click OK.

147

Run a Program with Elevated Privileges

If you need to perform advanced tasks in a program, you may need to run that program with elevated privileges.

Windows 8 implements a security model named *user account control* (UAC). The idea behind this security strategy is that you have permission to perform only a few day-to-day Windows tasks, such as moving and copying files. For more ambitious tasks that could affect the security of the system, Windows 8 asks you to provide credentials to prove that the task is not being performed by a virus program or other malicious software.

The credentials you provide depend on the type of account you have. If you have an administrator account, you click Yes in the

User Account Control dialog box; if you have a standard user account, you have to provide an administrator password.

However, this security model falls short when you need to perform certain actions. For example, if you edit a file in one of the Windows 8 protected folders, you receive a Permission Denied error when you try to save your changes.

To work around such problems, you need to start the program you are using with elevated privileges. This tells Windows 8 to run the program as though you were using the administrator account, which is the highest-level account on your system, and the only account that does not need to provide credentials.

① On the Start screen, type all or part of the name of the program you want to run elevated.

Ⓐ For example, to run the Command Prompt elevated, type **command**.

② Right-click the program in the search results (for example, Command Prompt).

③ Click Run as Administrator.

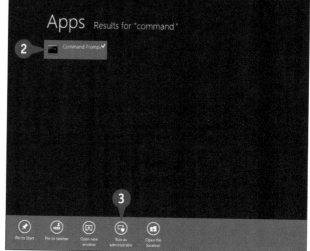

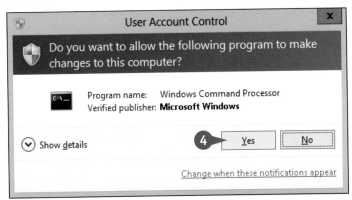

The User Account Control dialog box appears.

④ Click Yes.

If you have a standard user account, you must also type the password for an administrator account.

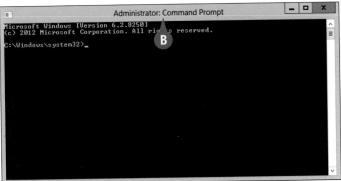

Ⓑ Windows 8 runs the program with elevated privileges.

TIPS

Did You Know?

If you have a program that you use frequently and you normally run it with elevated privileges, you can tell Windows 8 to always run the program elevated. Use File Explorer to find the file that runs the program, right-click the file, and then click Properties. Click the Compatibility tab, click the Run This Program as an Administrator check box (☐ changes to ☑), and then click OK. Note, however, that this technique does not work with the programs that come with Windows 8 (such as Command Prompt).

Caution!

When you run a program with elevated privileges, it not only enables you to perform otherwise forbidden tasks using the program, but the program itself can perform tasks that programs are usually prevented from doing (at least until you enter your credentials to allow them access to the system). Because elevated programs can perform forbidden tasks, only elevate privileges for programs you know and trust. Otherwise, you might inadvertently give a virus or Trojan horse program complete access to your system.

149

Run a Program in Compatibility Mode

If you are having trouble running an older program, you can customize the program's icon to run in compatibility mode so that it works properly under Windows 8.

For best performance and stability, you should try wherever possible to run programs that were designed only for Windows 8. This is not always practical, however, because it is likely that you have some programs that were released prior to Windows 8. Those older programs should run without any problems under Windows 8. However, this is not always the case.

The most common reason for such problems is that the older program was designed specifically to run under a particular operating system. For example, a program might have been designed for Windows 98 or Windows XP, and if the program encounters any other operating system, it either refuses to run or displays frequent glitches.

You can usually work around such problems by running the program in *compatibility mode*, where Windows 8 sets up an environment that mimics the operating system for which the program was designed.

---

① On the Start screen, type all or part of the name of the program you want to run.

② Right-click the program in the search results.

③ Click Open File Location.

Note: *If the program resides on a CD, DVD, or other removable media, use File Explorer to open the media.*

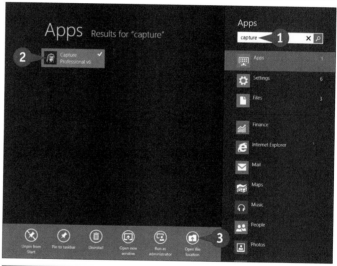

File Explorer displays the program file.

④ Click the Home tab.

⑤ Click Properties.

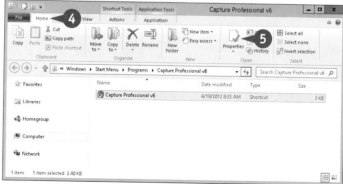

150

The program's Properties dialog box appears.

⑥ Click the Compatibility tab.

⑦ Click the Run This Program in Compatibility Mode For check box (☐ changes to ☑).

⑧ Click ▼ and then click the operating system for which the program was designed.

⑨ Click OK.

Windows 8 runs the program in compatibility mode each time you start it.

TIPS

More Options!
Some older programs do not run under Windows 8 because they require fewer colors than Windows 8 displays. For example, many older programs can use at most 256 (8-bit) or 65,536 (16-bit) colors, but the Windows 8 minimum is 16,777,216 colors. To fix this, follow steps 1 to 6, click the Reduced Color Mode check box (☐ changes to ☑), click ▼ and choose the number of colors, and then click OK.

More Options!
Another reason some older programs do not work with Windows 8 is because they expect a screen resolution of 640 x 480, and the minimum resolution under Windows 8 is 1024 x 768. To solve this problem, follow steps 1 to 6, click the Run in 640 x 480 Screen Resolution check box (☐ changes to ☑), and then click OK.

Boost Performance with a USB Flash Drive

If you add a USB flash drive to your computer, Windows 8 can use the storage space on that drive to improve the performance of your system.

Windows 8 uses a technology named SuperFetch to boost system performance. SuperFetch tracks the programs and data you use over time to create a kind of profile of your hard drive usage. Using this profile, SuperFetch can then anticipate the data that you might use in the near future. It can then load (fetch) that data into memory ahead of time. If that data is indeed what your system requires, performance increases because Windows 8 does not have to retrieve the data from your hard drive.

However, SuperFetch goes even further by also using Windows 8 ReadyBoost technology. If you insert a USB 2.0 or 3.0 flash drive (also called a memory key) into your system, Windows 8 asks you if you want to use the device to speed up your system. If you elect to do this, ReadyBoost uses that drive's capacity as storage for the data that SuperFetch anticipates you will require. This frees up the system memory that SuperFetch would otherwise use for storage, and more available memory means better performance for Windows 8 and your programs.

① Insert a flash drive into a USB port on your computer.

The AutoPlay notification appears.

② Click the notification.

Windows 8 displays a list of actions you can take with the flash drive.

③ Click Speed Up My System (using) Windows ReadyBoost.

Note: *If you do not see this option, it means your USB flash drive is not compatible with ReadyBoost.*

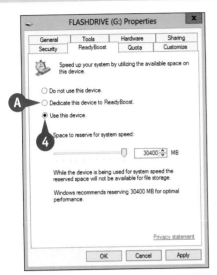

Windows 8 displays the ReadyBoost tab of the device's Properties dialog box.

④ Click Use This Device (○ changes to ◉).

Ⓐ If you want Windows 8 to use the entire drive for ReadyBoost, click Dedicate This Device to ReadyBoost, instead (○ changes to ◉), and then skip to step 5.

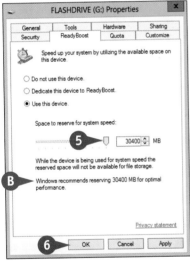

⑤ Click and drag the slider to set the amount of drive space Windows 8 sets aside for ReadyBoost.

Ⓑ You should set the drive space value to the value that Windows 8 recommends.

⑥ Click OK.

Windows 8 configures ReadyBoost to use the flash drive's memory.

TIPS

Did You Know?

If you have two USB flash drives and your computer has two available USB ports, you can insert both flash drives and tell Windows 8 to use them both to speed up your system. Keep in mind that you probably will not see much improvement in performance if your system has at least 2GB of RAM, because ReadyBoost does not need extra space when it has that much memory available.

Reverse It!

If you decide later on that you want to use the flash drive's full capacity for file storage, you can tell Windows 8 not to use the drive to augment ReadyBoost. Run File Explorer, click Computer, click the flash drive, click the Home tab, and then click Properties. Click the ReadyBoost tab and then click the Do Not Use This Device option (○ changes to ◉). Click OK to put the new setting into effect.

153

Terminate a Rogue App

You can make your system run faster as well as solve other problems by terminating apps that are unresponsive or that are taking up excess system resources.

Most apps — whether they are Windows 8 apps or desktop programs — run well most of the time. However, even the most finely crafted app might occasionally go rogue, meaning that it becomes unresponsive to mouse or keyboard input. If the app crashed really hard, it might cause systemwide instability or cause your other programs to run slowly.

Having an app go rogue might also mean that although it is still responsive, it is using up massive amounts of system resources, particularly CPU time or memory. In this scenario, the runaway app might cause your PC to run very slowly or it might cause other running programs to crash due to lack of available resources.

Whether you have an app that is unresponsive or is using up an inordinate amount of system resources, you can use Task Manager to terminate the app to maintain performance and to avoid destabilizing the entire system.

Display Task Manager

1. Right-click an empty section of the desktop.

A. The application bar appears.

2. Click All Apps.

3. Click Task Manager.

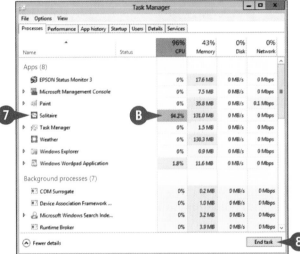

Terminate a Non-responsive App

④ Click the non-responsive app.

⑤ Click End Task.

Task Manager shuts down the app.

Terminate a Runaway App

⑥ Click More Details.

Ⓑ A runaway app is shown with an orange or red background to its CPU or Memory value.

⑦ Click the runaway app.

⑧ Click End Task.

Task Manager terminates the app.

TIPS

More Options!

You can also run Task Manager by pressing Windows Logo+X to display a menu of tools and programs, and then clicking Task Manager. Similarly, you can press Ctrl+Alt+Delete to display the Windows Security screen, and then click Task Manager. Finally, you can also type **task** and then click Task Manager in the search results.

Caution!

If an app is unresponsive, it is possible that it has crashed, but that is not guaranteed. For example, the app could just be really busy performing some task that takes an inordinately long time, such as recalculating a large spreadsheet or rendering a 3-D object. Therefore, you should always give an app a few minutes to see if it becomes responsive again on its own.

Refresh Your Computer's System Files

If you find that your computer is running slowly or that frequent program glitches and crashes are harming your productivity, you can often solve these problems by resetting your PC's system files.

System problems are often caused by misconfigured settings or corrupted files. You could spend hours trying to figure out which component or file is at fault, but Windows 8 offers a better way. The new Refresh Your PC feature reinstalls a fresh copy of Windows 8 while keeping your documents, settings, and Windows 8 apps intact. When you refresh your PC, Windows

8 copies this data to another part of the hard drive, reinstalls a fresh copy of the Windows 8 system files, and then restores your data.

Refresh Your PC saves all the documents, images, and other files in your user account, some of your settings, and any Windows 8 apps that you have installed. However, Refresh Your PC does *not* save any other PC settings (which are reverted to their defaults) or any desktop programs that you installed.

How you use Refresh Your PC depends on whether you can still access Windows 8 or whether you need to use a recovery drive.

Refresh Your PC from Windows 8

① On the Start screen, press Windows Logo+I.

The Settings pane appears.

② Click Change PC Settings.

The PC Settings app runs.

③ Click the General tab.

④ Click Get Started.

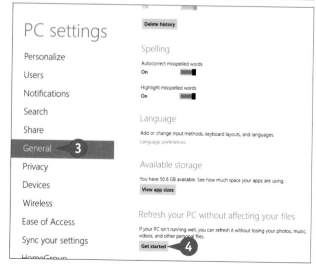

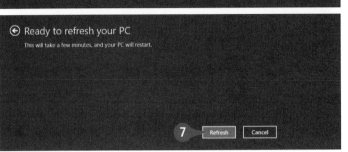

Refresh Your PC explains the process.

⑤ Insert your Windows 8 installation disc or a Windows 8 recovery drive.

⑥ Click Next.

⑦ Click Refresh.

Refresh Your PC reboots the computer and refreshes the system files.

TIPS

Caution!

Refresh Your PC begins the refresh process by making copies of all your user profile data, your settings, and your installed Windows 8 apps. These copies might take up a great deal of disk space, so you must have enough free space on your hard drive to hold this data. If you do not have enough space, you cannot refresh your PC.

Did You Know?

Refresh Your PC saves some of your settings, but not all of them. In particular, it saves your personalization settings, wireless network connections, mobile broadband connections, drive letter assignments, and BitLocker settings.

continued ▶

Refresh Your Computer's
System Files (continued)

If you cannot start Windows 8 because of a problem, you can still run Refresh Your PC from a Windows 8 recovery drive.

Some Windows problems are so severe that they prevent you from even starting your system. However, Windows 8 enables you to start your PC from another drive. In particular, you can start your PC using a Windows 8 recovery drive, which is a USB flash drive that contains special files

that can help you recover your system. You learn how to create a USB recovery drive in Chapter 11.

Once you start from the recovery drive, you enter the *recovery environment*, a special set of tools that help you recover from problems. One of these tools is Refresh Your PC, which enables you to reinstall Windows 8; this should fix the problem and get your system back on its feet.

Refresh Your PC from a Recovery Drive

1. Insert the recovery drive.

2. Restart your PC.

3. Boot to the recovery drive.

Note: *How you boot to the USB drive depends on your system.*

A. In some cases, you see a message telling you to press a key.

B. In some cases, you select a boot device from a menu.

The Windows 8 recovery environment appears.

Note: *If you see the Choose Your Keyboard Layout screen, click US.*

4. Click Troubleshoot.

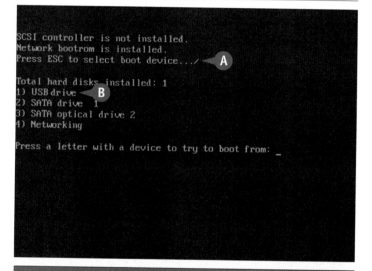

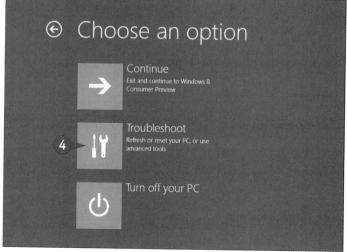

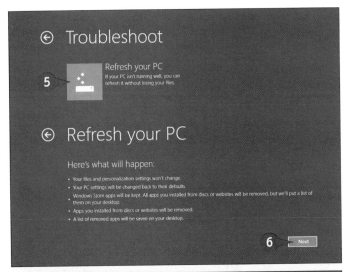

The Troubleshoot screen appears.

⑤ Click Refresh Your PC.

Refresh Your PC explains the process.

⑥ Click Next.

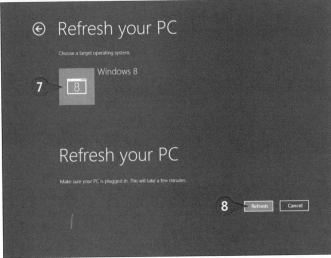

Refresh Your PC prompts you to choose a target operating system.

⑦ Click Windows 8.

⑧ Click Refresh.

Refresh Your PC reboots the computer and refreshes the system files.

TIP

More Options!

If you do not have a Windows 8 recovery drive, you can also run Refresh Your PC from your Windows installation media. Insert the media, restart your computer, and then boot to the media drive. When the Windows Setup dialog box appears, click Next, click Repair Your Computer, and then follow steps 4 to 8.

Tapping Into the Power of Internet Explorer

The World Wide Web is arguably the most impressive of the various services accessible via the Internet. With *billions* of pages available covering practically every imaginable topic, the web is one of our greatest inventions and an unparalleled source of information.

One problem with the web, though, is actually getting at all that information. With so much online ground to cover, you want a reliable and efficient means of transportation. For the World Wide Web, the vehicle of choice is the web browser, and in Windows 8, the default web browser is Internet Explorer, particularly the desktop version. This

program is fairly easy to use if all you do is click links and type website addresses. But to get the most out of the web, you can tap into the impressive array of features and options that Internet Explorer offers.

This chapter helps you do just that by taking you through a few useful tips and tricks that unleash the power of Internet Explorer. You learn how to take advantage of Internet Explorer's tabs feature, open multiple sites at startup, use your favorite search engine with Internet Explorer, save sites longer for easier surfing, view pop-up windows for specific sites, and more.

Add a Website to the Start Screen

You can customize the Start screen to give yourself easy access to websites that you use most often.

Because the Internet Explorer app takes only a single click to launch from the Start screen, you might find that you use it often for quick surfing sessions. Unfortunately, the surfing sessions probably are not as quick as you would like, because the Internet Explorer app does not offer a Favorites feature like that of desktop Internet Explorer.

Fortunately, the Internet Explorer app does come with a similar feature that enables you to pin websites as tiles on the Start screen. A quick click of a website tile, and the site loads automatically into the Internet Explorer app.

The Internet Explorer app also comes with a Pinned section within the app. Each time you pin a site to the Start screen, the Internet Explorer app also adds the site to the Pinned section for easy access within the app.

1 In the Internet Explorer app, surf to the site that you want to pin to the Start screen.

2 Click the Pin to Site icon.

3 Click Pin to Start.

4 Edit the website name.

5 Click Pin to Start.

The Internet Explorer app pins the website to the Start screen.

Note: *Click inside the Address box and then scroll right to see the Pinned section.*

Always Open Links in Desktop Internet Explorer

If you use the desktop version of Internet Explorer, you can configure it to always open Windows 8 app links as well as Start screen website tiles.

When you click a website link in a Windows 8 app such as Mail, People, or Messaging, by default Windows 8 opens the link using the Internet Explorer app. If you prefer to use desktop Internet Explorer, the only way to use that program to open the site is to copy the address from the Internet Explorer app and then

paste it to desktop Internet Explorer. This is cumbersome and inefficient, but you can avoid this by configuring your Internet options to always open Windows 8 app links in desktop Internet Explorer.

Also, in the previous section you learned how to add a website tile to the Start screen. By default, clicking a website tile opens the site in the Internet Explorer app; however, you can configure your Internet options to have those website tiles open in desktop Internet Explorer, instead.

1 In desktop Internet Explorer, click Tools.

2 Click Internet Options.

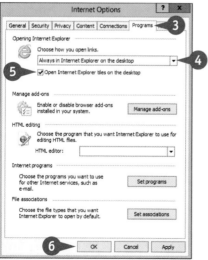

The Internet Options dialog box appears.

3 Click the Programs tab.

4 Click the Choose How You Open Links ⊡ and then click Always In Internet Explorer on the Desktop.

5 Click Open Internet Explorer Tiles on the Desktop (☐ changes to ☑).

6 Click OK.

Windows 8 now opens Windows 8 app links and website tiles in desktop Internet Explorer.

163

Disable an Internet Explorer Add-on

You can solve some Internet Explorer problems and make the program faster and more efficient by disabling one or more add-ons.

An *add-on* is an extra feature — such as a toolbar or a control — that does not come with Internet Explorer, but is installed separately. Although Microsoft offers some Internet Explorer add-ons, most come from third-party developers.

Add-ons can be extremely useful and can enhance not just Internet Explorer, but also your surfing experience. However, add-ons occasionally cause problems, either because they were not

programmed for the version of Internet Explorer you are using, or because there is a bug or other error in the add-on.

In such cases, the add-on may cause Internet Explorer to operate slowly, or it may cause the program to crash or fail to start. You can often fix this behavior by disabling the add-on that is causing the problem.

You may also want to disable an add-on that is cluttering the Internet Explorer window or otherwise interfering with your web surfing.

---

① Click Tools.

② Click Manage Add-ons.

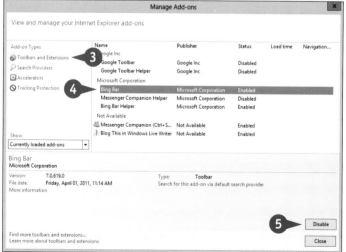

The Manage Add-ons dialog box appears.

③ Click Toolbars and Extensions.

④ Click the add-on you want to disable.

⑤ Click Disable.

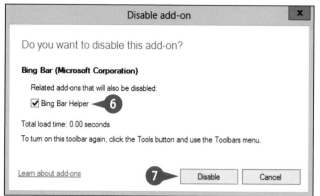

The Disable Add-on dialog box appears.

⑥ If you want to disable any other add-ons made by the same company, click the check box beside each add-on (☐ changes to ☑).

⑦ Click Disable.

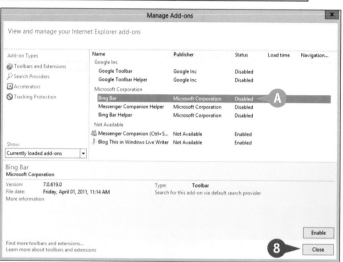

Ⓐ Internet Explorer changes the add-on's status to Disabled.

⑧ Click Close.

⑨ Shut down and restart Internet Explorer.

Internet Explorer does not load the disabled add-ons when it restarts.

TIPS

Try This!

If you are having problems with Internet Explorer, but you are not sure whether an add-on is at fault, try running the program without any add-ons. Press Windows Logo+R to open the Run dialog box, type **iexplore -extoff**, and then click OK. This runs Internet Explorer with all add-ons disabled. If Internet Explorer runs fine, you know an add-on is causing the problem.

Reverse It!

You may decide you want to use a disabled add-on again. For example, you may need the add-on's functionality, or you may realize that it is not causing any problems with Internet Explorer. To enable the add-on, follow steps 1 to 3, click the add-on, click Enable, and then click Enable again in the Enable Add-on dialog box.

Automatically Switch to New Tabs

You can make the Internet Explorer tab feature much more convenient by configuring the program to automatically switch to new tabs as you create them. Before Internet Explorer 7, if you wanted to open multiple websites at once, you had to open multiple copies of the Internet Explorer window.

Recent versions of Internet Explorer, including the version that comes with Windows 8, support *tabbed browsing*, which means you can open multiple websites at once in a single browser window. Each site appears in its own tab, and you can switch from one site to another just by clicking the tabs.

To open a site in a new tab, you right-click the link and then click Open in New Tab. Internet Explorer creates the tab and then opens the web page in the tab. However, to see the page, you must then click the tab. It is more efficient to have Internet Explorer automatically switch to a new tab when you create it.

---

1 Click Tools.

2 Click Internet Options.

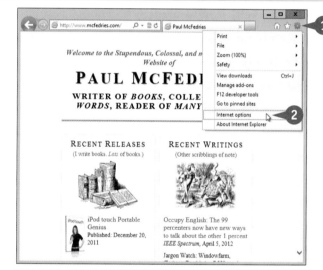

The Internet Options dialog box appears.

3 Click the General tab.

4 In the Tabs group, click Tabs.

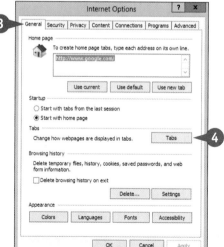

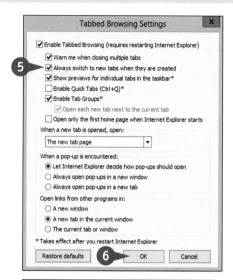

The Tabbed Browsing Settings dialog box appears.

5 Click the Always Switch to New Tabs when They Are Created check box (☐ changes to ☑).

6 Click OK.

7 Click OK.

The next time you create a tab, Internet Explorer automatically switches to it.

Open Multiple Pages When You Start Internet Explorer

If you regularly view several different pages at the start of each Internet Explorer session, you can save time by opening those pages automatically each time you start Internet Explorer.

In Internet Explorer, the *home page* is the page that the browser displays automatically when you first start the program. The default Internet Explorer home page is Bing.com, but most people change that to a page that they use regularly.

However, you may have more than one page that you open after Internet Explorer starts. For example, you may open a portal page such as MSN or Yahoo!, a search page such as Google, your company's external or internal website, a news page, one or more blogs, and so on. Opening each new tab and navigating to the appropriate page can take time.

The desktop version of Internet Explorer enables you to define multiple home pages. Internet Explorer automatically opens each home page in its own tab when you launch the program.

---

① Open the web page that you want to add as a home page.

② Right-click Home.

Ⓐ If you want to be able to access the Home Page list, activate the Command Bar toolbar.

③ Click Add or Change Home Page.

The Add or Change Home Page dialog box appears.

④ Click the Add This Webpage to Your Home Page Tabs option (○ changes to ◉).

⑤ Click Yes.

Ⓑ Internet Explorer adds the page to the Home list.

More Options!

If you do not currently have access to the Internet, you can still add a site as a home page. Click Tools (⚙) and then click Internet Options to display the Internet Options dialog box. In the General tab, click the last item in the Home Page list, press End, and then press Enter to start a new line. Type the address of the new home page and then click OK.

Remove It!

If you have set up a site as one of your Internet Explorer home pages, but you no longer visit that site, you should remove it to reduce the time it takes for Internet Explorer to launch. Click the Home menu, click Remove, and then click the home page that you want to delete. When Internet Explorer asks you to confirm, click Yes.

Open Previous Tabs When You Start Internet Explorer

You can pick up where you left off the last time you were using Internet Explorer by configuring the program to open the tabs that you were using during the previous session.

Tabbed browsing is a real boon to productivity because it enables you to keep several web pages open and easily accessible at once. This is particularly useful when you are working on a project where you need to be able to access several sites simultaneously. In many cases, it can take you quite a while to locate useful pages, close tabs for pages that are not useful,

and so on. This means you often end up with a "just so" collection of tabs that you want to use for a while.

This is a problem if you must then close Internet Explorer for some reason, because it means you lose all your tabs and you must then recreate them the next time you start a browsing session.

If this is a common scenario, you can solve the problem by configuring Internet Explorer to redisplay at startup all the tabs you had open in the previous session.

1 Click Tools.

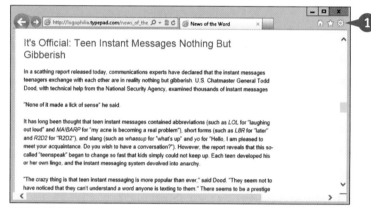

2 Click Internet Options.

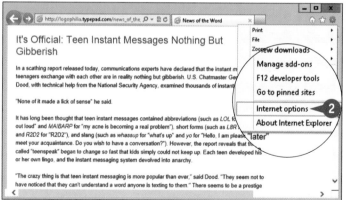

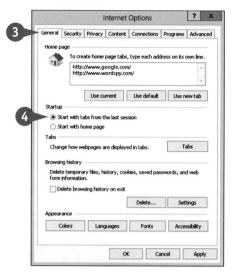

The Internet Options dialog box appears.

③ Click the General tab.

④ Click the Start with Tabs from the Last Session option (○ changes to ⊙).

⑤ Click OK.

The next time you start Internet Explorer, the program loads your previous tabs at startup.

TIPS

Caution!
Although opening your previous tabs at startup can be convenient, it can also increase the amount of time it takes Internet Explorer to start. Therefore, before you end each browsing session, examine your open tabs and close any that you will not need right away during your next session.

Try This!
If you regularly have a half dozen or more tabs open at once, the default position of the tabs — to the right of the Address bar — may be problematic because the tabs can become too small to be easily identifiable. To work around this problem, display the tabs on their own row. Right-click the Internet Explorer title bar and then click Show Tabs on a Separate Row.

Reset the Zoom Level for New Tabs

You can make it easier to use the Zoom feature in Internet Explorer by configuring the program to reset the zoom magnification each time you open a tab.

If your eyesight is impaired or just not what it used to be, you might use the Zoom feature to increase the magnification of the sites you visit. When you change the magnification for a page, Internet Explorer conveniently remembers the new setting and applies it to the next tab you open.

On the other hand, you might use the Zoom feature only occasionally. For example, you might use it to magnify the odd page that uses particularly small type. In this scenario, you likely do not want to use the same magnification for other pages, so when you open a new tab you must manually reset the Zoom level to 100 percent. To avoid this extra step, you can configure Internet Explorer to automatically reset the magnification for each new tab that you open.

---

1 Click Tools.

2 Click Internet Options.

The Internet Options dialog box appears.

3 Click the Advanced tab.

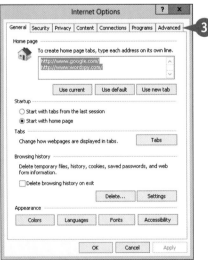

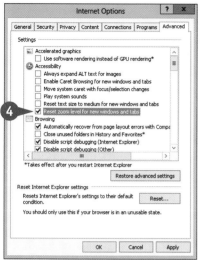

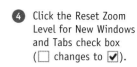 Click the Reset Zoom Level for New Windows and Tabs check box (☐ changes to ☑).

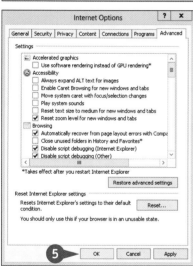

⑤ Click OK.

The next time you open a tab, Internet Explorer resets the Zoom level to 100 percent.

More Options

You may sometimes need to increase the text size to be able to read a page. (Press Alt, click View, click Text Size, and then click the size you want.) Again, Internet Explorer preserves the text size setting when you open a new tab. To prevent this, follow steps 1 to 3, click the Reset Text Size to Medium for New Windows and Tabs check box (☐ changes to ☑), and then click OK.

Did You Know?

If you prefer to keep the current magnification level each time you open a new tab, a quick way to reset the Zoom feature to 100 percent is to press Ctrl+0.

Navigate Tabs in the Order You Use Them

You can make it easier and more efficient to use the keyboard to navigate multiple tabs by configuring Internet Explorer to display the tabs in the order you have used them.

One way that tabs are very useful is to compare the content of two or more pages. That is, you open each page that you want to compare in its own tab, and you then display the tabs in turn to view the pages. It is possible to do this with the mouse by clicking each tab, but if you have a large number of tabs to navigate, the keyboard is usually the better choice. You simply press

Ctrl+Tab to navigate the tabs from left to right, or Shift+Ctrl+Tab to navigate the tabs from right to left.

Of course, this assumes the tabs you want to navigate are displayed in order. However, they are more likely to be mixed up, so that you might want to compare, say, the first, fourth, and sixth tabs, so clicking the tabs will be easier. Once you have done that, however, you can configure Internet Explorer so that pressing Ctrl+Tab (or Shift+Ctrl+Tab) navigates the tabs in the order you most recently used them.

---

1 Click Tools.

2 Click Internet Options.

The Internet Options dialog box appears.

3 Click the Advanced tab.

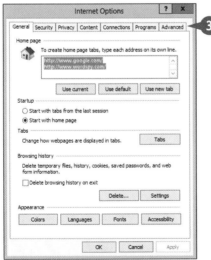

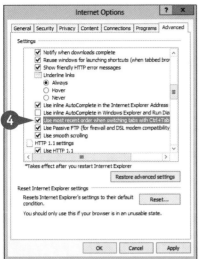

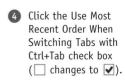 Click the Use Most Recent Order When Switching Tabs with Ctrl+Tab check box (☐ changes to ☑).

⑤ Click OK.

Internet Explorer now navigates the open tabs in the order you used them when you press Ctrl+Tab (or Shift+ Ctrl+Tab).

TIPS

Did You Know?

When you create a new tab from a link by right-clicking the link and then clicking Open in New Tab, Internet Explorer creates a *tab group* that consists of the original tab and the new tab. This enables you to close all the tabs in the group at once by right-clicking any tab in the group and then clicking Close This Tab Group.

More Options

When you open a new tab from a link, by default Internet Explorer opens the new tab beside the original one. This is very convenient, particularly if you have many tabs open, because it makes it easy to locate the new tab. If your version of Internet Explorer does not open new link tabs beside the original tab, click Tools (▦), click Internet Options, click Tabs, and then click Open Each New Tab Next to the Current Tab (☐ changes to ☑).

Improve Searching by Adding More Search Engines

You can make your web searches more powerful by adding your favorite search engines to the Internet Explorer Search box.

With billions of pages, the World Wide Web is an amazing information resource. However, it can also be a frustrating resource because *finding* the page you want among those billions is a real challenge. You can ask friends and family, or you can use a site such as Yahoo.com that categorizes pages, but these strategies are often unreliable.

To find the site you want, you can take advantage of the various search engines that

enable you to find web pages based on the search text you provide. The Internet Explorer Search box uses the Bing search engine to perform its searches.

If you prefer another search engine to Bing, you may decide that it is worth the extra effort to navigate to that site instead of using Bing via the Internet Explorer Search box. However, you can have it both ways: You can configure Internet Explorer to use your favorite search engine via the Search box.

---

1 Click the Show Address Bar Autocomplete arrow.

2 Click Add.

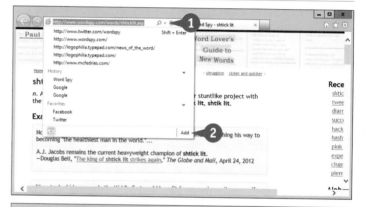

The Internet Explorer Gallery page appears.

3 Click the search engine you want to use.

Internet Explorer displays some information about the search engine.

④ Click Add to Internet Explorer.

The Add Search Provider dialog box appears.

⑤ Click Add.

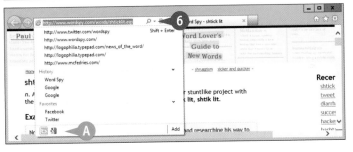

Internet Explorer adds the search engine.

⑥ Click the Show Address Bar Autocomplete arrow.

Ⓐ The new search engine appears in the Search list. Click the search engine to use it with the Search box.

TIPS

More Options!
The search engine that Internet Explorer uses in the Search box when you first start the program is called the *default search provider*. The default is Bing, but you can change it to one of your added search engines. Click Tools (⚙), click Manage Add-ons, and then click Search Providers. Click the search engine you want to use and then click Set as Default. Click Close.

Remove It!
If you add a search engine and later decide you do not want to use it, you should delete it to avoid cluttering the Search list. To remove a search engine, click Tools (⚙), click Manage Add-ons, and then click Search Providers. Click the search engine you want to delete and then click Remove. Click Close.

Save Websites Longer to Surf More Efficiently

You can improve the efficiency of your web surfing by increasing the number of days that Internet Explorer maintains a record of the sites you have visited.

When you navigate to a web page, Internet Explorer adds the page's title and address to the History list, which is part of the Favorites Center. The History list is an important Internet Explorer feature because it enables you to easily and quickly return to a page that you have previously visited. The History list also enables

you to view the pages that you have visited most often, so it gives you an easy way to see which pages are your favorites.

By default, Internet Explorer keeps a page in the History list for 20 days before removing it. However, you may find that you want to revisit pages after the 20-day period has expired. In that case, you can configure Internet Explorer to save pages in the History list for a longer period. The maximum number of days you can save pages is 999.

1 Click Tools.

2 Click Internet Options.

The Internet Options dialog box appears.

3 Click the General tab.

4 In the Browsing History group, click Settings.

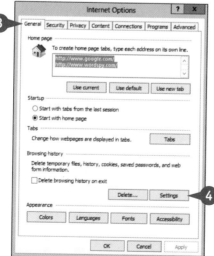

The Website Data Settings dialog box appears.

⑤ Click the History tab.

⑥ Use the Days to Keep Pages in History spin box to type or click the number of days you want websites saved.

⑦ Click OK.

⑧ Click OK.

Internet Explorer puts the new setting into effect.

Try This!

To work with the History list, click the Favorites button (⭐) and then click History. (You can also press Ctrl+H.) The History list organizes your visited sites into date categories such as Today, Yesterday, Last Week, and Last Month. Click a category, click the site you want to work with, and then click the specific page you want to visit.

Did You Know?

You can sort the History list in various ways. The default sort order is By Date. To change this, display the Favorites Center, click the History menu, and then click View By Site, View By Most Visited, or View By Order Visited Today. You can also click Search History to perform a search on the history entries.

Always Check for Newer Versions of Web Pages

You can ensure that you are always seeing the most up-to-date version of each web page by configuring Internet Explorer to always check for newer versions of its stored pages.

In the same way that a disk cache stores frequently used data for faster performance, Internet Explorer also keeps a cache of files from web pages you have visited recently. This cache is a special folder called Temporary Internet Files. When you visit a page, Internet Explorer stores copies of the web page code, images, and other media in Temporary Internet Files. Internet Explorer then uses these saved files to display that web page quickly the next time you surf to the page or if you view the page while you are offline.

However, there is a chance that the web page may have changed since your last visit, so Internet Explorer may show the older version of the page. To prevent this from happening, configure Internet Explorer to always check to see if the current page files are newer than the stored page files.

1 Click Tools.

2 Click Internet Options.

The Internet Options dialog box appears.

3 Click the General tab.

4 In the Browsing History group, click Settings.

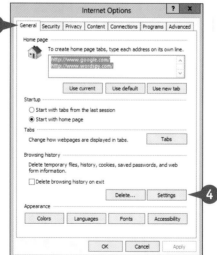

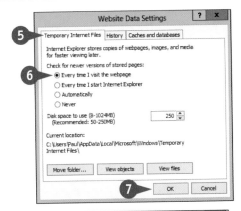

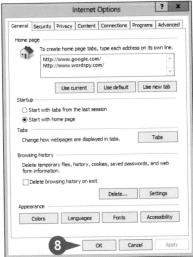

The Website Data Settings dialog box appears.

⑤ Click the Temporary Internet Files tab.

⑥ Click the Every Time I Visit the Webpage option (○ changes to ●).

⑦ Click OK.

⑧ Click OK.

Internet Explorer puts the new setting into effect.

TIPS

More Options!
If you have a lot of free disk space, you can make your surfing even faster by configuring Internet Explorer to cache more data in the Temporary Internet Files folder. Follow steps 1 to 5 to open the Temporary Internet Files tab of the Website Data Settings dialog box, and then use the Disk Space to Use spin box to increase the size of the cache.

More Options!
If your computer has a second hard drive and your main hard drive is running low on free space, you can move the Temporary Internet Files folder to the second drive. Follow steps 1 to 5 to open the Temporary Internet Files tab of the Website Data Settings dialog box, and then click Move Folder. Use the Browse for Folder dialog box to select a folder on the second hard drive, and then click OK.

View Pop-Ups from a Specific Website

You can improve your surfing experience by configuring Internet Explorer to view the pop-up ads for certain websites that Internet Explorer would otherwise block.

Web page advertising is a necessary evil because webmasters often need the money from advertisers to help defray the inevitable costs of maintaining a site. Banner ads are a popular choice, but to make more of an impact, advertisers often insist that their ads appear in separate pop-up windows. These pop-ups are everywhere on the web these days. Small personal pages may display a single pop-up when you enter or leave the site; some commercial sites display a few pop-ups as you peruse their pages; and then there are those sites that throw out a barrage of pop-ups. Depending on your level of tolerance, pop-ups are either mildly irritating or downright annoying. Either way, pop-up ads can make surfing the web a real chore.

However, some sites display useful information in pop-up windows, and Internet Explorer may block these windows. If so, you can add the site's address to the list of sites allowed to display pop-ups.

① Click Tools.

② Click Internet Options.

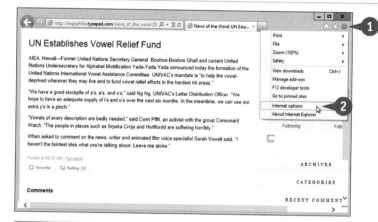

The Internet Options dialog box appears.

③ Click the Privacy tab.

④ In the Pop-Up Blocker section, click Settings.

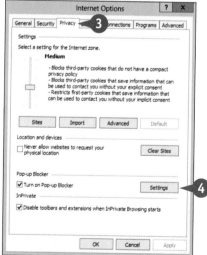

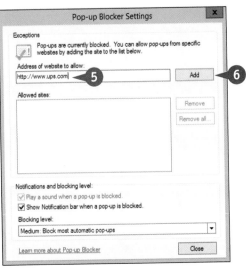

The Pop-Up Blocker Settings dialog box appears.

5 Type the site address in the Address of Website to Allow text box.

6 Click Add.

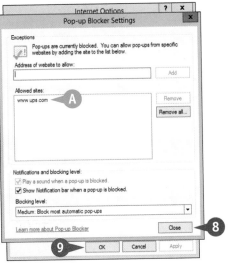

A Internet Explorer includes the address in the Allowed Sites list.

7 Repeat steps 5 and 6 to add other sites to the Allowed Sites list.

8 Click Close.

9 Click OK.

10 Restart Internet Explorer.

The next time you visit the site, Internet Explorer displays its pop-up windows.

TIPS

More Options!
Instead of typing a site's address in the Pop-Up Blocker Settings dialog box, an easier method is to navigate to the site and look for the Internet Explorer Information bar that appears when the program blocks a pop-up. If you only want to see the pop-ups this time, click Allow Once. To always see the site's pop-ups, click Options for This Site and then click Always Allow.

More Options!
If you only want to occasionally allow pop-ups from a site, follow steps 1 to 4, use the Blocking Level list to click High: Block All Pop-Ups, and then click Close. The next time you navigate to the site and want to view its pop-ups, press and hold Ctrl and Alt until the pop-up appears.

Turn On the Menu Bar by Default

You can make Internet Explorer much easier to use and more efficient by always displaying the menu bar.

Internet Explorer is a powerful program with hundreds of commands and features. However, the default interface exposes only a subset of those options, mostly via the Tools button. Unfortunately, this subset does not include a number of useful commands, including New Session (which starts a fresh Internet Explorer session), Import and Export (for importing or exporting browser settings), Source (which

displays the source code of the current page), Text Size (for adjusting the size of the web page text), and Pop-Up Blocker (for quick access to the pop-up blocker settings).

These and many more commands *are* available via the menu bar, which many users find easier to use than the Tools menu. Users can display the menu bar at any time by pressing Alt. However, you can configure your system so that Internet Explorer always displays the menu bar and the user cannot turn it off.

---

1 Sign in with the user account you want to configure.

2 Press Windows Logo+R.

The Run dialog box appears.

3 Type **gpedit.msc**.

4 Click OK.

The Local Group Policy Editor appears.

5 Open the Administrative Templates branch.

6 Open the Windows Components branch.

7 Click Internet Explorer.

8 Double-click the Turn On Menu Bar by Default policy.

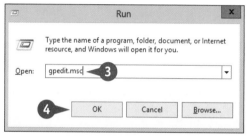

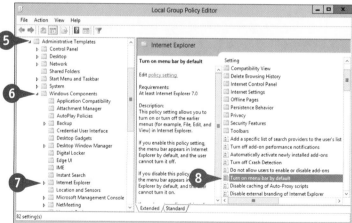

184

The Turn On Menu Bar by Default dialog box appears.

9 Click Enabled
(○ changes to ◉).

10 Click OK.

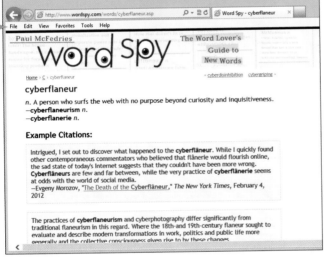

11 Restart Internet Explorer.

A The menu bar appears.

Customize the Favorites Bar for Easier Surfing

You can customize the Internet Explorer Favorites bar to provide easy one-click access to those websites that you visit most often.

One of the most useful features in Internet Explorer is the Favorites bar, which appears beside the Favorites button. By default it consists of two buttons, each of which is associated with a web slice. When you click a button, Internet Explorer displays the Get More Add-Ons slice and the Suggested Sites slice.

However, the Favorites bar is fully customizable and supports not only web slices, but also regular sites. This means you can populate the Favorites bar with new buttons associated with the sites you visit most often. This section takes you through these and other Favorites bar customizations.

This section assumes that you have the Favorites bar displayed. If not, right-click the title bar and then click to activate the Favorites Bar command.

Create a Button for the Current Web Page

1. Navigate to the page you want to add to the Favorites bar.

2. Click Add to Favorites Bar.

A. A new button associated with the page appears on the Favorites bar. You can click this button to navigate directly to the page.

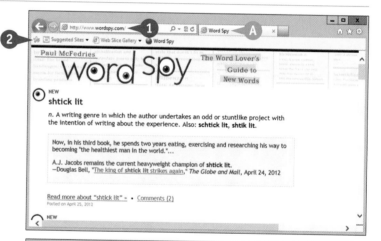

Create a Button from a Web Page Link

1. Navigate to the page that contains the link you want to add to the Favorites bar.

2. Click and drag the link text and drop it on the Favorites bar.

A new button associated with the linked page appears on the Favorites bar. You can click this button to navigate directly to the linked page.

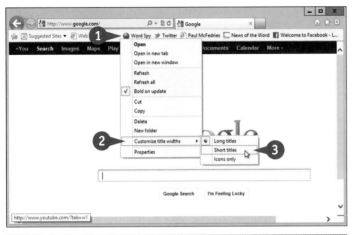

Customize the Title Widths

1 Right-click any Favorites bar button.

2 Click Customize Title Widths.

3 Click the width you prefer, such as Short Titles.

B Internet Explorer customizes the Favorites bar titles.

Customize It!

The positions of the Favorites bar buttons are not fixed. To move a button to another position, click and drag the button and then drop it in the position you prefer. To rename a button, right-click it, click Rename, type the new name in the Rename dialog box, and then click OK. To delete a button, right-click it, click Delete, and then click Yes when Internet Explorer asks you to confirm the deletion.

Did You Know?

If the address of one of your sites changes, you can edit the address associated with the site's Links bar button. Right-click the button and then click Properties. In the button's Properties dialog box, type the new address in the URL text box. Click OK.

Chapter 8

Making E-Mail Easier

The World Wide Web may be the most impressive of the Internet services, but it would not be hard to make the case that e-mail is the most indispensable. E-mail's position midway between conversation and letter writing makes it ideal for certain types of communication, and rarely can a person be found nowadays who does not rely on it.

The fact that e-mail is easy to use also helps. Even novice computer users seem to grasp the basics of e-mail quickly and are often sending messages within minutes. But if, like most people, you use e-mail all day long, you probably want to make it

even easier. This chapter shows you how to do that. The tasks you learn here are designed to shave precious seconds and minutes off everyday e-mail chores. That may not sound like much, but added up over the course of a busy e-mail day, those seconds can make the difference between leaving work on time and staying late.

Among the timesavers in this chapter, you learn how to leave messages on the server, change your message priority, create an e-mail distribution list, create a backup copy of your address book, exchange electronic business cards, and spell check your messages.

Leave Your Messages on the Server

You can configure Mail to leave your messages on the server, enabling you to retrieve a message multiple times from different computers.

When you ask Mail to retrieve your messages, it contacts your Internet service provider's e-mail server, downloads the messages, and then deletes them from the server. However, there may be times when you do not want the messages deleted. For example, if you are working at home or on the road and want to

retrieve your work messages, it is better to leave them on the server so that you can also retrieve them when you return to the office.

Note, however, that most Internet service providers (ISPs) offer a limited amount of e-mail storage space, so you cannot leave messages on the server indefinitely. To ensure that your messages are deleted eventually, you can configure your account to delete your messages from the server after a specified number of days.

---

1 In Mail, click the account you want to configure.

2 Click the Accounts tab.

3 Click Properties.

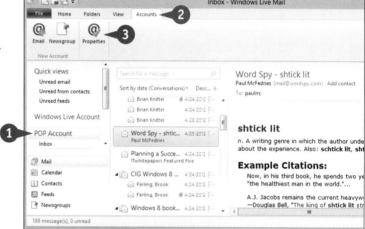

The account's Properties dialog box appears.

4 Click the Advanced tab.

5 Click the Leave a Copy of Messages on Server check box (☐ changes to ☑).

Ⓐ To ensure the messages are deleted eventually, you can click the Remove from Server After *x* Days check box (☐ changes to ☑) and then change *x* to the number of days after which you want the server messages deleted.

6 Click OK.

Mail leaves a copy of the messages on the server.

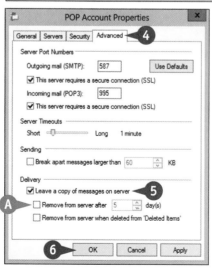

You can set the priority level of your outgoing message to let the recipient know whether to handle your message with high or low priority.

If you are sending a message that has important information or that requires a fast response, set the message's priority to high. When the recipient receives the message, his or her e-mail program indicates the high priority. For example, Mail indicates high priority messages with a red exclamation mark. Alternatively, you can set the priority to low for unimportant messages so that

the recipient knows not to handle the message immediately. Mail flags low priority messages with a blue, downward-pointing arrow.

If you are sending important information via e-mail, you may want to ensure that the message arrived safely. You can do that by sending a request for a *read receipt*, which is a message that is automatically sent to you when the recipient reads the message for the first time (although many people do not allow read receipts to be sent, for privacy reasons).

1 In Mail, click the Home tab.

2 In the New group, click Email Message.

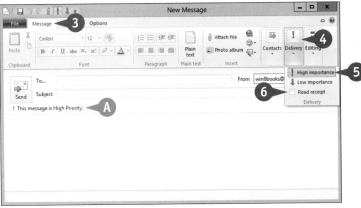

The New Message window appears.

3 Click the Message tab.

4 Click Delivery.

5 Click the priority you want to use: High or Low.

Ⓐ Mail indicates the current priority level.

6 If you want to request a read receipt, click the Read Receipt check box (☐ changes to ☑).

191

E-Mail Multiple People Using a Contact Category

If you regularly send messages to a particular collection of people, you can organize those recipients into a category. This saves time because when you choose the category as the message recipient, Mail sends the message to every address in the category.

Sending a message to a number of people takes time because you have to either type many addresses or select many people from your address book. If you find that you are sending

some of your messages to the same group repeatedly, you can avoid the drudgery of adding those recipients individually by creating a distribution list or, as Mail calls it, a *contact category*.

After you add the recipients to the list, all you have to do is send the message to the category. Mail then distributes copies of the message to every member of the category.

---

① In Mail, click Contacts.

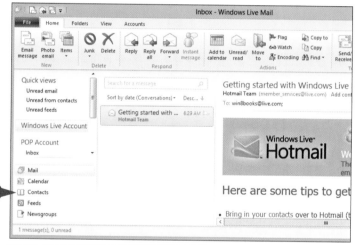

The Contacts window appears.

② In the Home tab's New group, click Category.

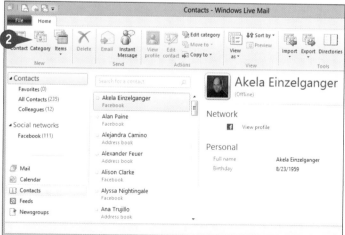

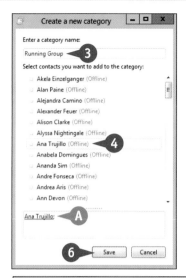

The Create a New Category window appears.

3 Type a name for the category.

4 Click a contact that you want to include in the category.

A Contacts adds the contact to the category.

5 Repeat step 4 for the other contacts you want to add to the category.

Note: *If you add the wrong contact by accident, you can remove it by clicking the contact name again.*

6 Click Save.

B Contacts adds the category.

TIPS

Try This!

One of the best reasons to create a category is that you can send an e-mail message to each member. Normally, sending an e-mail message to multiple contacts involves typing or selecting multiple addresses. With a category, however, you send a single message to the category, and Mail automatically sends a copy to each member. In a new mail message, use the To text box to type the name of the category.

More Options!

If you want to add new contacts to the category or delete existing contacts, click the category and then click Edit Category. If you want to delete a category, right-click the category and then click Delete Category. When Contacts asks you to confirm the deletion, click OK.

Protect Your Contacts by Creating a Backup Copy

You can create a backup copy of your contacts. If you have a problem with the contacts in the future, you can restore your contacts from the backup copy.

Contacts is handy for storing e-mail addresses of people you correspond with regularly. Instead of remembering complex e-mail addresses, you can type or select the person's name when composing a new message. However, the usefulness of Contacts extends far beyond e-mail. For each contact, you can also store data

such as his or her home and business addresses; phone, fax, and cell numbers; spouse and children's names; gender; birthday; and more.

If you rely on Contacts to store all this information about the people you know, you must ensure that the data is safe. Unfortunately, if Contacts becomes corrupted, you could lose all your contact data. To avoid this situation, you can regularly create backup copies of your Contacts data.

1 In Mail, click Contacts.

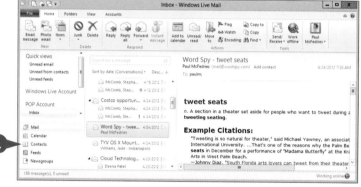

The Contacts window appears.

2 Click Export.

3 Click Comma Separated Values (.CSV).

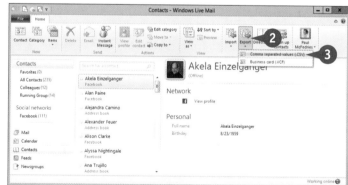

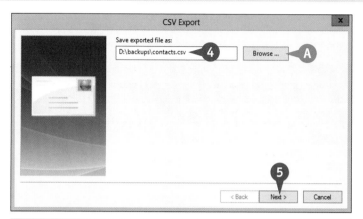

The CSV Export dialog box appears.

④ Type the location and name of the exported file.

Note: *Be sure to add .csv to the end of the exported filename.*

Ⓐ You can also click Browse and use the Save As dialog box to select a location and type a filename.

⑤ Click Next.

⑥ Click the check boxes for each field you want to include (☑) or exclude (☐).

⑦ Click Finish.

Mail exports the Address Book data to the file.

TIPS

Important!

If you have a problem with your Contacts folder — for example, if it does not open or does not display your contacts — you can restore it by importing the backed-up copy. In Mail, click Contacts, click Import, and then click Comma Separated Values (.CSV). Type the location and name of the exported file from step 4 and click Next. Click Finish.

Did You Know?

You can also make backup copies of your Mail messages and e-mail accounts. Click File and then click Export Email. To back up your e-mail messages, click Email Messages, click Mail, and then click Next; to back up your accounts, click Accounts, click an account, and then click Export.

E-Mail an Electronic Business Card

You can create an electronic version of a business card that includes your name, address, and contact information. You can then attach this business card to your messages, enabling other people to easily add you to their address books.

The ritual exchange of business cards is a common sight at meetings, conferences, and cocktail parties. With the advent of e-mail, however, fewer people are meeting face-to-face, so there are fewer opportunities to swap cards. Fortunately, Mail offers a feature that enables you to exchange business cards electronically.

An electronic business card is called a *vCard* and, just like its paper counterpart, it includes the person's name, address, phone numbers, and other contact information. If you have an item in the Contacts folder for yourself, you can use it to create a vCard, which you can then attach to your messages. The recipient can then view the attached card and easily add you to his or her address book. Similarly, you can view vCards sent to you and add the senders to your Contacts list.

Create Your Electronic Business Card

1. In Mail, click Contacts.

   The Contacts window appears.

   Note: *If you do not have a contact with your personal data, create one now.*

2. Click the Home tab.

3. Click Export.

4. Click Business Card (.VCF).

   The Browse for Folder dialog box appears.

5. Click your user profile's Contacts folder.

6. Click OK.

   Contacts exports the contacts to VCF files in the Contacts folder.

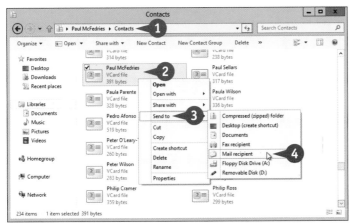

Send Your Electronic Business Card

1. Open your user account's Contacts folder.

2. Right-click your vCard.

3. Click Send To.

4. Click Mail Recipient.

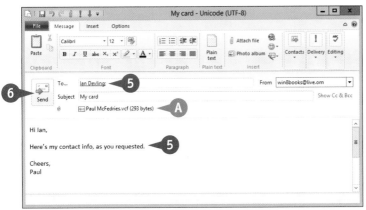

Mail displays a new message window.

Ⓐ Your electronic business card file is attached to the new message.

5. Fill in the message details, including the recipient, subject, and message text.

6. Click Send.

Mail sends the message with your electronic business card attached.

TIPS

Try This!
You can also add your business card directly from an e-mail message that you are composing. In the e-mail message window, click Attach to display the Open dialog box. Navigate to the Contacts folder, click your vCard file, and then click Open.

Did You Know?
If you receive a message that includes a vCard, you can see the business card icon (▦) in the preview pane. Click the icon and then click Open to open the attached vCard file. To add the sender to your Contacts list, click Add Contact.

Change the Location of Your Message Store

You can change the hard drive location that Mail uses to store the contents of your message folders. This is useful if you are running out of space on the current hard drive and need to move the messages to a disk with more free space.

Mail stores the contents of your Inbox, Outbox, Sent Items, Deleted Items, Drafts, and Junk E-mail folders, as well as any new folders you create, in a special hard drive location called the *message store*. The size of the message store depends on a number of factors, including how often you use e-mail, how many messages you save, how often you clean out your Deleted Items folder, and so on.

However, it is not unusual for the message store to consume dozens or even hundreds of megabytes of disk space. If you are running low on disk space and your computer has another hard drive with more free space, you can give your message store room to grow by moving it to the other disk.

1 In Mail, click File.

2 Click Options.

3 Click Mail.

The Options dialog box appears.

4 Click the Advanced tab.

5 Click Maintenance.

The Maintenance dialog box appears.

6 Click Store Folder.

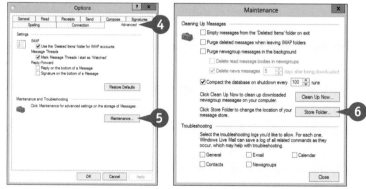

The Store Location
dialog box appears.

⑦ Click Change.

The Browse for Folder
dialog box appears.

⑧ Click the folder you
want to use as the new
location.

⑨ Click OK to close the
Browse for Folder dialog
box.

⑩ Click OK to close the
Store Location dialog
box.

Mail tells you to shut
down the program to
put the new store
location into effect.

⑪ Click OK.

⑫ Click Close to close the
Maintenance dialog
box.

⑬ Click OK to close the
Options dialog box.

⑭ Click Close to shut down
Mail and then restart
the program.

Mail moves the message
store.

TIPS

Important!
To speed up the process of moving the
message store, you can do some folder
maintenance before performing these steps.
For example, delete any messages you no
longer want, including any messages in the
Deleted Items folder. You can also delete any
folders that you no longer use.

More Options!
Another way to save disk space with Mail is to
compact your folders to remove wasted space
caused by message deletions. Follow steps 1 to
5 to display the Maintenance dialog box. Use
the Compact the Database on Shutdown Every
X Runs spin box to specify a relatively small
number of runs, such as 10 or 20; the default
is 100. Click Close and then click OK.

Activate the Spell Checker to Eliminate Message Errors

You can make your e-mail messages easier to read and more professional in appearance by using the Mail built-in spell checker to catch and fix spelling errors.

Whether you use e-mail for short notes or long essays, you can detract from your message if your text contains more than a few spelling errors. Sending a message riddled with spelling mistakes can also reflect poorly on you, whether the recipient is your boss, your colleagues, a customer, or a recruiter.

To ensure your message is received in its best light, you should activate the Mail spell checker. This tool then checks your text for errors each time you send a message and offers suggested replacements.

You can also improve the spell checker by letting it know about flagged words that you know are correct. This can happen with people's names, company names and products, jargon terms, and so on.

1 Click File.

2 Click Options.

3 Click Mail.

The Options dialog box appears.

4 Click the Spelling tab.

5 Click the Always Check Spelling Before Sending check box (☐ changes to ☑).

6 Click OK.

Mail activates the spell checker.

Note: *During a spell check, if Mail flags a word that you know is correct, you can prevent it from flagging the word in the future by clicking Add in the Spelling dialog box.*

Change How Often You Check for Messages

After you start Mail, the program contacts your mail server every 10 minutes to see if any new messages have arrived. You can change the frequency with which Mail checks for new messages to any time between 1 minute and 480 minutes. For example, you may prefer a shorter time if you are expecting an important message. Alternatively, if you want to minimize your connection time, you may prefer a much longer interval.

You can also configure Mail to automatically connect to the Internet to check messages. This is useful if you set your e-mail checking frequency to a value higher than the Internet connection idle time setting. In this scenario, your Internet connection may be disconnected when Mail tries to check for new messages, but Mail can make the connection.

1. Click File.
2. Click Options.
3. Click Mail.

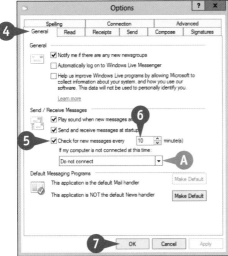

The Options dialog box appears.

4. Click the General tab.

5. Click Check for New Messages Every (☐ changes to ☑).

6. Type the frequency, in minutes, with which you want to check for messages.

Ⓐ To connect to the Internet to check for messages, click here and then click Connect Even When Working Offline.

7. Click OK.

Mail puts the new setting into effect.

Perform an Action When a Person Sends You a Message

You can save time and make Mail more useful by configuring the program to perform an action each time you receive a message from a particular person.

In Mail, you use rules to examine incoming messages to see if they meet certain conditions. For example, if a message has a particular word or phrase in the Subject line or body, you can move the message to a special folder. Similarly, you can check for messages with attachments and elect not to download them from the mail server.

Perhaps the most common rule condition is to see if the e-mail address of the sender matches a specified address. If so, then you can redirect the message to a folder for that person's messages, send out an automatic reply, turn the message a particular color so that it stands out, or even automatically delete the message if it comes from someone with whom you do not want to have contact.

① If the person is not in your Contacts list, right-click the sender and then click Copy.

② Click the Folders tab.

③ Click Message Rules.

The New Mail Rule dialog box appears.

④ Click Where the From Line Contains People (☐ changes to ✔).

⑤ Click Contains People.

⑥ Press Ctrl+V to paste the sender's address.

Ⓐ You can also click Contacts to choose the person from your Contacts list.

⑦ Click Add.

⑧ Click OK.

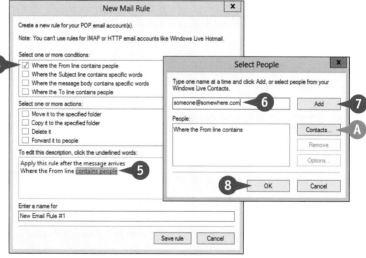

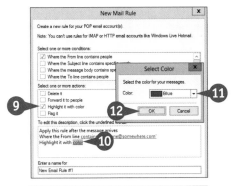

⑨ Click an action to perform on messages from this person (☐ changes to ☑).

⑩ If the action requires more data, click the underlined placeholder.

Mail displays a dialog box so you can specify a value for the placeholder. Note that the dialog box you see depends on the action you chose in step 9.

⑪ Click the data (or, in some cases, type the text) to set the placeholder value.

⑫ Click OK.

Ⓑ Mail fills in the placeholder value.

⑬ Type a name for the rule.

⑭ Click Save Rule.

Mail opens the Rules dialog box and displays the new rule.

⑮ Click OK.

TIPS

Apply It!
After you create the rule from the message, Mail does not apply the rule right away. To apply the rule, open the Rules dialog box, if it is not already open, by clicking Folders and then clicking Message Rules. In the Rules dialog box, click Apply Now, click the rule you created, and then click Apply Now.

Remove It!
If you no longer require a rule, you can delete it. Click Folders and then click Message Rules to display the Rules dialog box. Click the rule and then click Remove. When Mail asks you to confirm the deletion, click Yes.

Change Your Outgoing Mail Port to Ensure Messages Are Sent

If your e-mail provider requires a different port for outgoing mail, you can configure your e-mail account to use the different port so that your message is sent.

For security reasons, some Internet service providers (ISPs) insist that all their customers' outgoing mail must be routed through the ISP's Simple Mail Transport Protocol (SMTP) server. This usually is not a big deal if you are using an e-mail account maintained by the ISP, but it can lead to several problems if you are using an account provided by a third party (such as your website host). For example, your ISP might block messages sent using the third-party account

because it thinks you are trying to relay the message through the ISP's server (a technique that spammers often use).

You might think that you can solve the problem by specifying the third-party host's SMTP server in the account settings. However, this usually does not work because outgoing e-mail is sent by default through port 25, and your ISP automatically blocks all messages on this port that leave the ISP's network; when you use this port, you must also use the ISP's SMTP server.

To work around this problem, many third-party hosts offer access to their SMTP server via a port other than the standard port 25.

① Click the account you want to configure.

② Click the Accounts tab.

③ Click Properties.

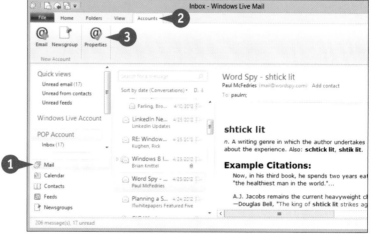

The account's Properties dialog box appears.

④ Click the Advanced tab.

⑤ Use the Outgoing Mail (SMTP) text box to type the server port you want to use for outgoing messages.

⑥ Click OK.

Mail uses the new port for all future outgoing messages.

Receive E-Mail Notification for an Incoming Fax

If you use Windows Fax and Scan to receive incoming faxes, you can configure the program to send you a delivery receipt as an e-mail message each time a fax comes in.

If you receive faxes, Windows Fax and Scan is a handy program because you can configure it to automatically answer incoming fax calls. Windows Fax and Scan then displays a message telling you that a new fax has been received.

However, if Windows Fax and Scan is running on a PC other than the one you are using, you might not be in a position to see the new fax message. Instead of constantly checking the other PC for a new fax, Windows Fax and Scan has an option that enables you to have a delivery notification sent to an e-mail address that you specify. You can also configure Windows Fax and Scan to attach a copy of the fax to the e-mail message.

① On the Start screen, type **fax**.

② Click Windows Fax and Scan.

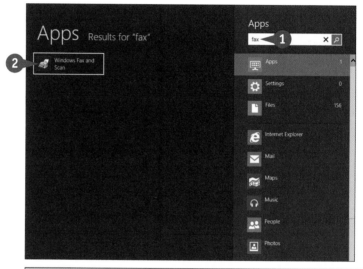

The Windows Fax and Scan window appears.

③ Click Tools.

④ Click Options.

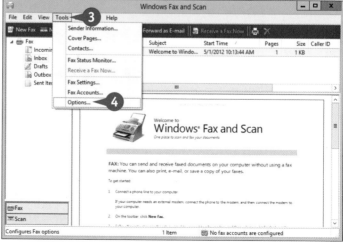

The Fax Options dialog box appears.

5 Click the Receipts tab.

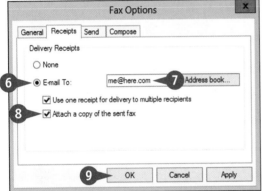

6 Click E-mail To (○ changes to ●).

7 Type the e-mail address where you want the notification sent.

8 Click Attach a Copy of the Sent Fax (□ changes to ☑).

9 Click OK.

With each newly received fax, Windows Fax and Scan now e-mails you a notification and a copy of the fax.

TIPS

Important!
Before you use Windows Fax and Scan, you should create a fax account. In Windows Fax and Scan, click Tools, click Fax Accounts, click Add, click Connect to a Fax Modem, click Next, and then click Answer Automatically (or use a different answering setting, if you prefer). If you see the Windows Security dialog box, click Allow Access, and then click Close.

More Options!
Now that you are receiving fax notifications, you might want to disable the sounds that Windows Fax and Scan makes when it receives a fax. Click Tools and then click Fax Settings to open the Fax Settings dialog box. Click the Tracking tab and then click Sound Options to open the Sound Settings dialog box. Click An Incoming Call Rings (☑ changes to □), click A Fax Is Received (☑ changes to □), and then click OK.

Chapter

9

Enhancing Internet Security and Privacy

The Internet is now the online home away from home for more than two billion people around the world. The lure of all that information, entertainment, and camaraderie has proven to be simply impossible to resist.

But the Internet has also lured more than its fair share of another class of people: malicious hackers, system intruders, and con artists of every stripe. These miscreants seem to spend most of their waking hours thinking up new ways to disrupt the Internet, break into your online computer, and steal everything from your credit card number to your full identity.

Thankfully, like crime in the real world, online crime is still relatively rare. However, as the newspaper headlines attest almost daily, cybercrime is a big business, and so it pays to play it safe.

This chapter helps by offering you a full suite of tasks and techniques designed to make your Internet sessions as safe as possible. You learn how to remove saved website passwords, delete your browsing history, prevent ad sites from tracking you online, prevent sites from requesting your location, use e-mail safely and securely, and control junk e-mail.

You can avoid unauthorized access to a website by removing the site's password that you saved earlier using Internet Explorer.

Many World Wide Web sites require registration to access certain pages and content. In almost all cases, before you can navigate to any of these restricted pages, you must first enter a password, along with your username or e-mail address. When you fill in this information and log on to the site, Internet Explorer displays the AutoComplete dialog box and offers to remember the password so that you do not have to type it

again when you visit the same page in the future. If you click Yes and then access the site's login page at a later date, Internet Explorer fills in the password for you automatically.

This is convenient, to be sure, but it has a downside: Anyone who uses your computer can also access the password-protected content. If you do not want this to happen, one solution is to click No when Internet Explorer asks to remember the password. Alternatively, you can tell Internet Explorer to remove the saved password, as described in this section.

① Press Windows Logo+W.

The Settings search pane appears.

② Type **credential**.

③ Click Manage Web Credentials.

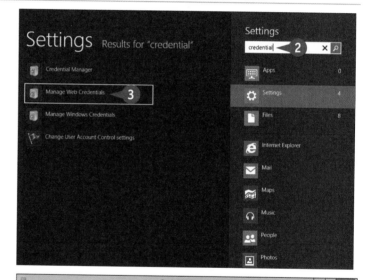

The Credential Manager window appears.

④ Click the web password you want to remove.

Credential Manager displays the site details.

5 Click Remove.

Credential Manager asks you to confirm the deletion.

6 Click Yes.

Credential Manager removes the password.

TIPS

Important!

Many websites offer to "remember" your login information. They do this by placing your username and password in a small file called a *cookie* that is stored on your computer. Although convenient, it may lead to a problem: Other people who use your computer can access the password-protected content. To avoid this, be sure to click the check box that asks if you want to save your login data (☑ changes to ☐).

Did You Know?

If you have several login passwords stored on your computer, you may want to delete them all. Rather than going through them individually, follow the steps shown in the "Delete Your Browsing History to Ensure Privacy" section, and be sure to click the Passwords check box (☐ changes to ☑).

211

Delete Your Browsing History to Ensure Privacy

To ensure that other people who have access to your computer cannot view information from sites you have visited, you can delete your browsing history.

As you visit websites, Internet Explorer maintains information about the sites you visit. Internet Explorer also maintains a folder called Temporary Internet Files that stores copies of page text, images, and other content so that sites load faster the next time you view them. Similarly, Internet Explorer also saves the names of files you have downloaded as well as text and passwords that you have typed into forms.

Internet Explorer also maintains *cookies*, which are small text files that store information such as site preferences and site logon data.

Saving all this data is useful because it enables you to quickly revisit a site. However, it is also dangerous because other people who use your computer can just as easily visit or view information about those sites. This can be a problem if you visit financial sites, private corporate sites, or some other page that you would not want another person to visit. You reduce this risk by deleting some or all of your browsing history.

① Click Tools.

② Click Safety.

③ Click Delete Browsing History.

Note: *You can also press Ctrl+Shift+Delete.*

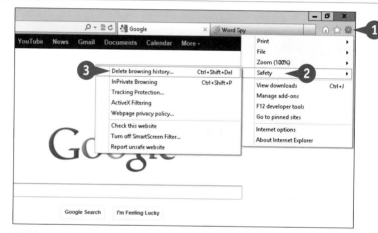

The Delete Browsing History dialog box appears.

④ To keep the browsing history associated with sites on your Favorites list, click Preserve Favorites Website Data (☐ changes to ✔).

⑤ To delete saved web page files, click Temporary Internet Files and Website Files (☐ changes to ✔).

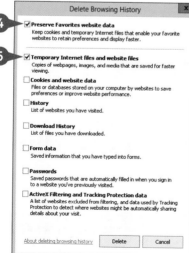

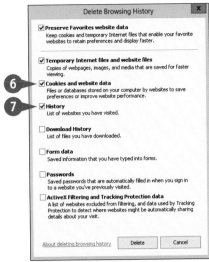

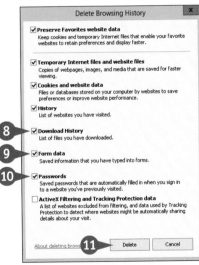

⑥ To delete cookie files and website data, click Cookies and Website Data (☐ changes to ✔).

⑦ To delete the list of websites you have visited, click History (☐ changes to ✔).

⑧ To delete the list of files that you have downloaded, click Download History (☐ changes to ✔).

⑨ To delete saved form data, click Form Data (☐ changes to ✔).

⑩ To delete saved form passwords, click Passwords (☐ changes to ✔).

⑪ Click Delete.

Internet Explorer deletes the selected browsing history.

TIPS

Try This!

If you visit a site that you do not want to save cookies to your computer, you can block that site. To do this, click Tools (⚙) and then click Internet Options. In the Internet Options dialog box, click the Privacy tab and then click Sites to open the Per Site Privacy Actions dialog box. Type the site address and then click Block. Click OK.

More Options!

If you regularly delete all your browsing history, constantly running the Delete Browsing History command can become tiresome. Fortunately, you can configure Internet Explorer to make this chore automatic. Click Tools (⚙) and then click Internet Options to display the Internet Options dialog box. Click the General tab, and then click the Delete Browsing History on Exit check box (☐ changes to ✔). Click OK.

Turn On Private Browsing

If you visit sensitive or private websites, you can tell Internet Explorer not to save any browsing history for those sites.

In the previous section you learned that Internet Explorer saves a great deal of data as your surf the web. This data includes temporary Internet files, website data, cookies, surfing history, downloads, form data, and site passwords. If you regularly visit private websites or websites that contain sensitive or secret data, you can ensure that no one else sees any data for these sites by deleting your browsing history.

However, if these sites represent only a small percentage of the places you visit on the web, deleting your entire browsing history is overkill. A better solution is to turn on the InPrivate Browsing feature in Internet Explorer before you visit private sites. This tells Internet Explorer to temporarily stop saving any browsing history. When you are ready to surf regular websites again, you can turn off InPrivate Browsing to resume saving your browsing history.

① Click Tools.

② Click Safety.

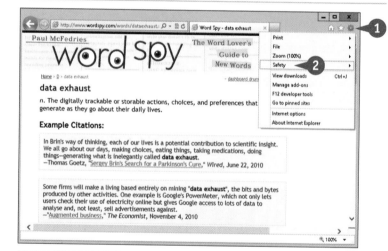

③ Click InPrivate Browsing.

Note: *You can also activate the InPrivate Browsing command by pressing Ctrl+Shift+P.*

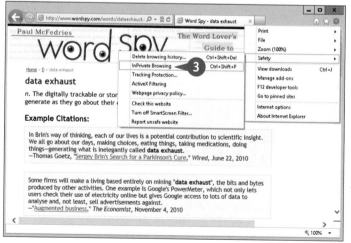

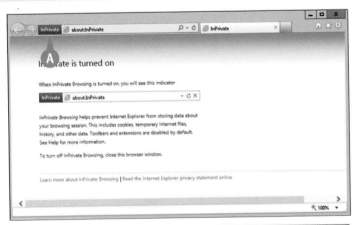

Internet Explorer opens a new window and activates InPrivate Browsing.

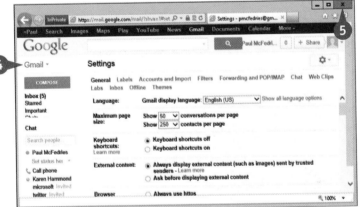

Ⓐ The InPrivate indicator tells you that InPrivate Browsing is turned on.

④ Visit the sites you want to see during your private browsing session.

⑤ When you are done, click Close to close the window and turn off InPrivate Browsing.

Prevent Ad Sites from Tracking You Online

You can prevent advertising sites from tracking your online movements by blocking the tracking files that they store on your PC.

A *cookie* is a small text file that is stored on your computer by a website that needs to "remember" information about your session at that site: shopping cart data, page customizations, usernames, passwords, and so on.

No other site can access your cookies, so they are generally safe and private under most — but definitely not all — circumstances. To understand why cookies can sometimes compromise your privacy, you have to understand the difference

between the two main cookie types: a *first-party cookie* is a cookie set by the website you are viewing; a *third-party cookie* is a cookie set by a site other than the one you are viewing. An ad site might store information about you in a third-party cookie and then use that cookie to track your online movements and activities. The advertiser can do this because it might have an ad on dozens or hundreds of websites, and that ad is the mechanism that enables the site to set and read their cookies.

To prevent this, you can configure Internet Explorer to block third-party cookies.

---

① Click Tools.

② Click Internet Options.

The Internet Options dialog box appears.

③ Click the Privacy tab.

④ Click Advanced.

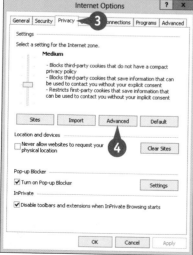

The Advanced Privacy Settings dialog box appears.

⑤ Click Override Automatic Cookie Handling (☐ changes to ☑).

⑥ Under Third-Party Cookies, click Block (○ changes to ◉).

⑦ Click OK.

⑧ Click OK.

Internet Explorer no longer accepts cookies from third-party sites.

TIPS

More Options!
You might find that disabling third-party cookies causes some websites to load improperly or not at all. This usually means that the site requires information from a third party, but that information cannot get through because the third party cannot set a cookie. You might be able to work around this problem by allowing *session cookies*, which exist only during the current Internet Explorer session. Follow steps 1 to 5 and then click Always Allow Session Cookies (☐ changes to ☑).

Remove It!
If you find that you still cannot use many of your regular sites properly with third-party cookies blocked, you might be better offer returning to Internet Explorer's automatic cookie handling. Follow steps 1 to 3 and then click Default.

Enable and Configure Tracking Protection

You can get more fine-grained protection against being tracked online by enabling the Tracking Protection feature in Internet Explorer and configuring it to suit your needs.

Blocking third-party cookies, as described in the previous section, is a useful starting point for preventing your online activities from being tracked. However, the sites you visit might also use other types of content from third-party sites, such as maps, web analytical tools, and, of course, advertisements. Most of this content is benign, but some of it could give a third party access to some of your personal data.

To prevent this, Internet Explorer implements Tracking Protection, which is the web equivalent of a "Do Not Call" list for telephone solicitors. If you block third-party content — that is, you configure that content with a kind of "Do Not Track" label — then Internet Explorer prevents any site from requesting that content from the third party.

Once you enable Tracking Protection, Internet Explorer begins monitoring the websites you visit, looking for third-party content. After a piece of content is accessed a specific number of times (the default value is 10), Internet Explorer adds it to your personal Tracking Protection List (TPL), where you can then block it, if desired.

Enable Tracking Protection

1. Click Tools.
2. Click Safety.
3. Click Tracking Protection.

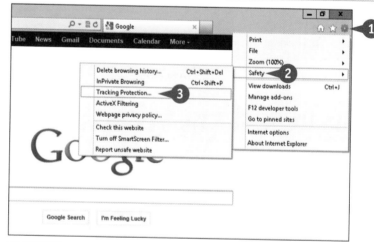

The Manage Add-ons dialog box appears with the Tracking Protection section displayed.

4. Click Your Personalized List.
5. Click Enable.
6. Click Close.

Internet Explorer turns on Tracking Protection and begins monitoring the sites you visit for third-party content.

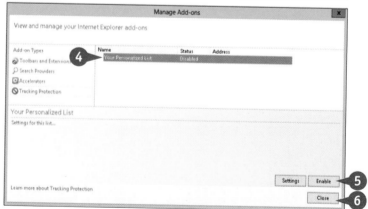

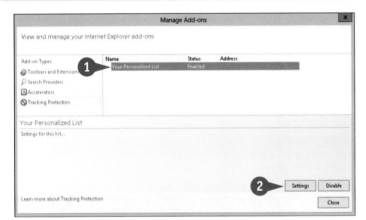

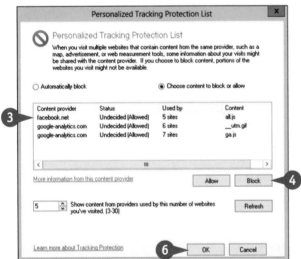

Configure Tracking Protection

1 Follow steps 1 to 4 in the previous set of steps to select Your Personalized List.

2 Click Settings.

Internet Explorer displays the content that it has added to your TPL.

3 Click the content you want to block.

4 Click Block.

5 Repeat steps 3 and 4 for each piece of content you want to block.

6 Click OK.

TIP

Add It Automatically!

If you find that managing your TPL becomes burdensome, you can let other people handle the task for you. Microsoft has authorized users and companies to put together custom TPLs that automatically block known tracking sites, such as advertisers.

To add a TPL, follow steps 1 to 3 in the first set of steps to display the Tracking Protection section and then click Get a Tracking Protection List Online. This displays the TPL section of the Internet Explorer Gallery site. If you see a TPL that looks useful, click the Add button beside it, and then click Add List when Internet Explorer asks you to confirm.

To view the list, double-click it in the Tracking Protection section. Note, too, that you can add more than one TPL for added protection.

Prevent Sites from Requesting Your Location

You can enhance your privacy by preventing websites from tracking your physical location.

If you have a computer, particularly a tablet PC, that has a built-in Global Positioning System (GPS) receiver, it can pinpoint your location to within a few feet. Even if you have a basic PC that does not include GPS technology but does include Wi-Fi, a website can still get a fix on your current location by examining the known wireless access points in your surrounding area.

All this means that it is possible for websites to determine your current location. For example, if you ask Google maps for directions to an address, it defaults to using your current location as the starting point. When this happens, Internet Explorer displays an Information bar that asks you to give permission to the site to track your location. You can then deny the request.

If you would rather not have any websites tracking your location, you can disable this feature. You can also clear any sites that you have allowed to access your location.

Prevent a Site from Requesting Your Location

1. In the Information bar, click Options for This Site.

2. Click Always Deny and Don't Tell Me.

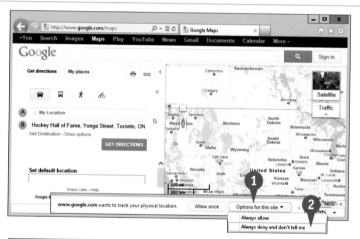

Prevent All Sites from Requesting Your Location

1. Click Tools.

2. Click Internet Options.

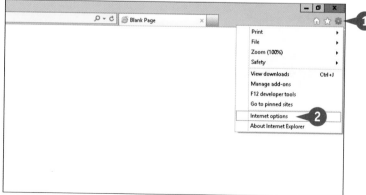

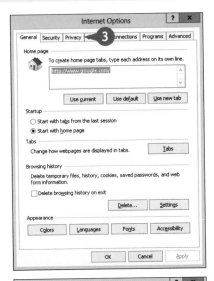

The Internet Options dialog box appears.

③ Click the Privacy tab.

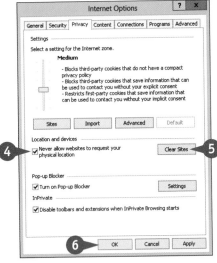

④ Click Never Allow Websites to Request Your Physical Location (☐ changes to ☑).

⑤ To revoke permission from any previous sites, click Clear Sites.

⑥ Click OK.

Internet Explorer no longer prompts you when a website requests your location.

TIP

More Options!
The desktop version of Internet Explorer is not the only Windows 8 app that can request your location. For example, when you first launch the Maps app or the Weather app, Windows 8 asks you in each case whether the app can use your location. To prevent any apps from requesting your location, press Windows Logo+I to open the Settings pane, click Change PC Settings, click Privacy, and then click the Let Apps Use My Location switch to Off.

Play Web Page Media
Safely and Privately

You can set options in Windows Media Player that ensure media downloaded from or played on an Internet site is safe, and that enhance the privacy of the Internet media you play.

You can play Internet media either by downloading the music or video to your computer and playing it in Windows Media Player, or by using a version of Windows Media Player that resides inside a web page. Either way, the person who created the media may have included extra commands in a script

designed to control the playback. Unfortunately, scripts can also contain commands that harm your computer, so preventing these scripts from running is the best option.

Also, Windows Media Player stores the names of media files that you play and the addresses of websites that you visit to access content. If other people use or have access to your computer, you may want to enhance your privacy by not allowing Windows Media Player to store this history.

---

① In Windows Media Player, click Organize.

② Click Options.

The Options dialog box appears.

③ Click the Security tab.

④ Click the Run Script Commands and Rich Media Streams When the Player Is in a Web Page check box (☑ changes to ☐).

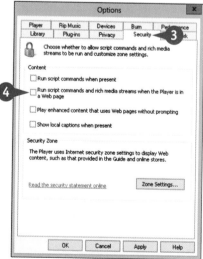

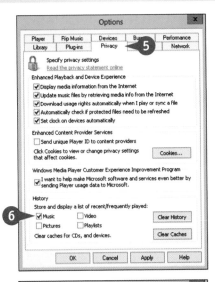

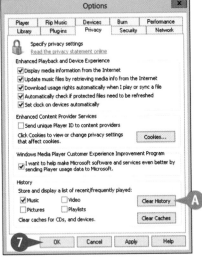

5 Click the Privacy tab.

6 In the History section, click the check box for each type of media you do not want to appear in the Windows Media Player history list (☑ changes to ☐).

A If you want to clear the existing history list, click Clear History.

7 Click OK.

Windows Media Player puts the new security and privacy options into effect.

Thwart E-Mail Viruses by Reading Messages in Text

You can reduce the danger of accidentally unleashing a virus on your computer by reading all your e-mail messages in text format.

E-mail messages come in two formats: plain text and HTML. The HTML format utilizes the same codes used to create web pages. Therefore, just as some web pages are unsafe, so are some e-mail messages. Specifically, messages can contain scripts that run automatically when you open or even just preview a message. You can prevent these scripts from running by viewing all your messages in the plain text format.

When you are viewing a message as plain text, you may realize that the message is innocuous and that it is okay to view the HTML version. To switch quickly to HTML, press Alt+Shift+H.

---

① Click File.

② Click Options.

③ Click Mail.

The Options dialog box appears.

④ Click the Read tab.

⑤ Click Read All Messages in Plain Text (☐ changes to ☑).

⑥ Click OK.

E-mail messages now appear only in plain text.

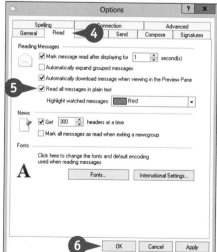

Thwart Web Bugs by Blocking Images in Messages

You can make your e-mail address more private by thwarting the web bugs inserted into some e-mail messages.

A *web bug* is a small and usually invisible image, the code for which is inserted into an e-mail message. That code specifies a remote address from which to download the web bug image when you open or preview the message.

However, the code also includes a reference to your e-mail address. The remote server makes note of the fact that you received the message, which means your address is a working one and is therefore a good target for further spam messages. By blocking web bugs, you undermine this confirmation and so receive less spam.

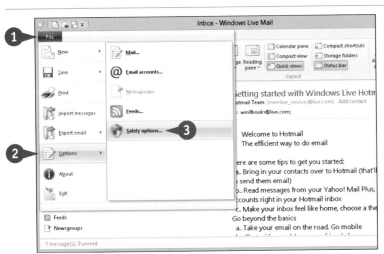

1 Click File.

2 Click Options.

3 Click Safety Options.

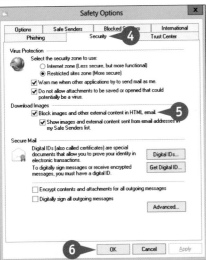

The Safety Options dialog box appears.

4 Click the Security tab.

5 Click Block Images and Other External Content in HTML E-mail (☐ changes to ☑).

6 Click OK.

Windows blocks images and other external content in HTML e-mail.

Note: *To see the images in a legitimate e-mail message, press F9 or click Show Images above the message header in the Reading pane.*

Eliminate Spam by Using the Safe Senders List

If you have a junk e-mail problem that feels out of control, you can eliminate all spam from your Inbox by using Mail's Safe Senders list.

Mail normally marks a message as junk if it detects spam characteristics within the message. A different approach is to set up a *whitelist* of allowable addresses. Mail offers such a whitelist: the Safe Senders list. If a person's address (such as someone@somewhere.com) or an organization's domain (such as somewhere.com) is on the Safe

Senders list, then Mail never treats messages from that person or domain as spam.

If you add all your contacts to the Safe Senders list, then you can configure the Mail junk e-mail protection level to accept messages only from people or domains in the Safe Senders list. All other messages are marked as spam.

Note, too, that by default, Mail also trusts e-mail from people in your Contacts list.

① In Mail, click File.

② Click Options.

③ Click Safety Options.

The Safety Options dialog box appears.

④ Click the Options tab.

⑤ Click Safe List Only (○ changes to ◉).

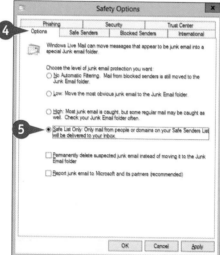

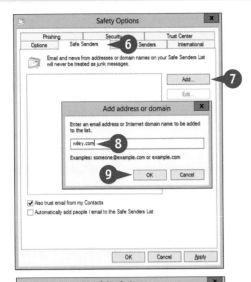

6 Click the Safe Senders tab.

7 Click Add.

The Add Address or Domain dialog box appears.

8 Type an address or domain that you want to include in your Safe Senders list.

9 Click OK.

Ⓐ Mail adds the address to the list.

10 Repeat steps 7 to 9 as necessary.

Ⓑ Leave this check box activated (☑) so that Mail also trusts your Contacts.

11 Click OK.

Mail now only delivers messages from your safe senders to your Inbox, and it marks all other messages as spam.

Note: *If you find a legitimate message in your Junk Email folder, click it and then click the Home tab's Not Junk button.*

TIPS

Try This!

If you have messages from some or all of the people or domains you want to include in your Safe Senders list, Mail gives you an easier way to add them. Right-click a message, click Junk Email, and then click Add Sender to Safe Senders List. For the domain name, click Add Sender's Domain to Safe Senders List, instead.

More Options!

You can configure Mail to automatically add to your Safe Senders list anyone to whom you send a reply or an original message. Follow steps 1, 2, 3, and 6 to display the Safe Senders tab, and then click Automatically Add People I Email to the Safe Senders List (☐ changes to ☑). Click OK.

Add a Person to Your Blocked Senders List

If you receive spam or other unwanted messages from a particular person, you can configure Mail to block that person's address so that you do not have to see or deal with messages from that person again.

Spam messages are most often sent with fake return addresses that change with each message. However, it often happens that a particular person sends junk messages using a legitimate return e-mail address. In this case, you can add that address to the Mail Blocked Senders list.

Any future messages from that person — as well as any messages from that person currently in your Inbox folder — are automatically rerouted to the Junk Email folder.

However, the Blocked Senders list is not just for spam. If you have a person who is sending you annoying, insulting, or offensive messages, you can add that person's address to the Blocked Senders list. Again, Mail automatically moves that person's messages to the Junk Email folder so you do not have to deal with them.

① In Mail, click File.

② Click Options.

③ Click Safety Options.

The Safety Options dialog box appears.

④ Click the Blocked Senders tab.

⑤ Click Add.

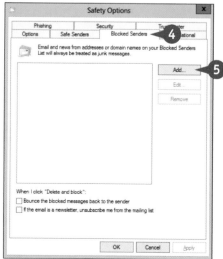

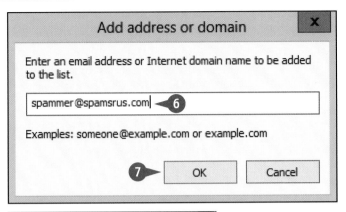

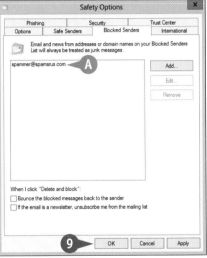

The Add Address or Domain dialog box appears.

⑥ Type the address of the person you want to block.

⑦ Click OK.

Ⓐ Mail adds the address to the Blocked Senders list.

⑧ Repeat steps 5 to 7 to add more addresses to your Blocked Senders list.

⑨ Click OK.

When you receive messages from any of the people you added to the Blocked Senders list, Mail moves those messages to the Junk Email folder.

TIPS

Try This!

Some spammers use varying addresses that change the username but keep the same domain name — for example, sales@spammer.com, offers@spammer.com, and so on. To block all messages from this type of spammer, add just the domain name — @spammer.com in this example — to the Blocked Senders list.

More Options!

If you have a message from a person you want to block, right-click the message and then click Junk Email. In the menu that appears, click either Add Sender to Blocked Senders List or Add Sender's Domain to Blocked Senders List.

Block Messages from a Country to Reduce Spam

If you receive a great deal of spam from e-mail addresses that originate in a particular country, you can avoid dealing with those messages by telling Mail to block messages that come from that country.

On the Internet, a *domain name* is a name that specifies an Internet location. The main domain name takes the form mydomain.com, and most domains also have subdomains such as a website (usually www.mydomain.com) or a mail server (usually mail.mydomain.com).

The part of the domain name after the last dot is called the top-level domain, and some, such as

com, edu, and org, are not country-specific. However, many top-level domains do use country or region codes. For example, ca is the top-level domain for Canada, uk is for Great Britain, de is for Germany, and us is for the United States.

If you find that you are getting many spam messages from addresses that use a top-level domain for a particular country, you can configure Mail to block messages from these domains. Any future messages from that country — as well as any messages from that country currently in your Inbox folder — are automatically moved to the Junk Email folder.

---

1 In Mail, click File.

2 Click Options.

3 Click Safety Options.

The Safety Options dialog box appears.

4 Click the International tab.

5 Click Blocked Top-Level Domain List.

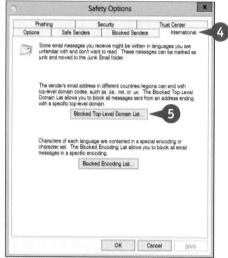

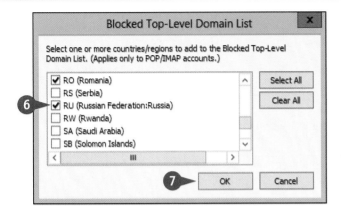

The Blocked Top-Level Domain List dialog box appears.

⑥ Click the check box for each country you want to block (☐ changes to ☑).

⑦ Click OK.

⑧ Click OK.

Mail begins blocking messages from the country or countries you selected.

If any of the messages in your Inbox folder come from the blocked countries, Mail moves those messages to the Junk Email folder.

<hr>

TIPS

More Options!
If you want to block messages from all foreign countries with just a few exceptions, activating most of the check boxes in the Blocked Top-Level Domain List dialog box can be time-consuming. An easier method is to click Select All to activate every check box and then click to uncheck the countries you do not want blocked (☑ changes to ☐).

Try This!
If you regularly get messages written in a different language that you do not understand, you should treat these messages as junk e-mail. To configure Mail to block these messages, follow steps 1 to 4 and then click Blocked Encoding List. In the Blocked Encodings List dialog box, click the check box for each language you want to block (☐ changes to ☑), and then click OK.

Automatically Move Phishing Messages to the Junk Mail Folder

You can avoid dealing with phishing messages by configuring Mail to automatically move all phishing messages to the Junk Email folder.

Phishing refers to creating a replica of an existing web page to fool a user into submitting personal, financial, or password data. The term comes from the fact that Internet scammers are using increasingly sophisticated lures as they "fish" for users' financial information and password data. The most common ploy is to copy the web page code from a major site — such as

AOL or eBay — and use it to set up a replica page that appears to be part of the company's site. (This is why another name for phishing is *spoofing*.)

Phishing usually begins with a scammer sending out a fake e-mail message with a link to this page, which solicits the user's credit card data or password. Mail looks for phishing messages and automatically blocks links and other content in those messages, but it does not automatically move those messages to the Junk Email folder.

---

① In Mail, click File.

② Click Options.

③ Click Safety Options.

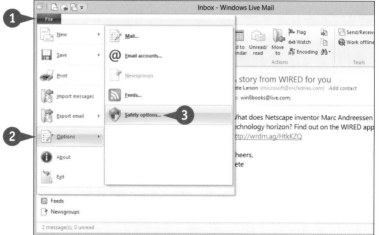

The Safety Options dialog box appears.

④ Click the Phishing tab.

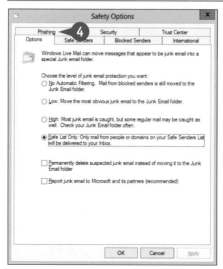

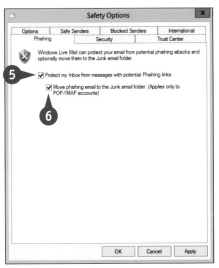

5 Make sure the Protect My Inbox from Messages with Potential Phishing Links check box is activated (☑).

6 Click Move Phishing Email to the Junk Email Folder (☐ changes to ☑).

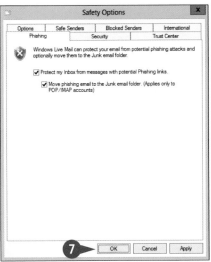

7 Click OK.

If you receive any phishing messages, Mail moves those messages to the Junk Email folder.

TIPS

Caution!

Although Mail does a decent job of recognizing phishing messages, it sometimes creates false positives: legitimate messages that Mail has mistakenly marked as phishing messages and moved to the Junk Email folder. Therefore, you should check your Junk Email folder more often to look for legitimate messages.

Did You Know?

To help you avoid phishing websites, the desktop version of Internet Explorer 10 comes with a tool called the SmartScreen Filter. This filter alerts you to potential phishing scams by analyzing the site content for known phishing techniques, and by checking a global database of known phishing sites. The filter is on by default. To make sure, click Tools (⚙) and then click Safety. If you see the Turn On SmartScreen Filter command, click it and then click OK.

Prevent Mail from Sending a Read Receipt

You can block Mail from sending a message that confirms you have opened a message.

The Internet e-mail system occasionally breaks down and some e-mail messages never arrive at their destination. Often you get no indication that there was a problem, so you assume the message got through.

A person sending an important message may want to know whether you have read the message because then at least they know the message was delivered safely. A *read receipt* is a short message that Mail automatically fires back

to the sender when you open or preview a message from that person. The read receipt — which must be requested by the sender — ensures the sender that you have viewed the message. However, many people consider this an invasion of privacy, so they block Mail from sending read receipts.

By default, Mail displays a dialog box that tells you the sender has requested a read receipt. You can block read receipts either by declining to send one each time Mail asks or by blocking read receipts entirely.

Prevent a Single Read Receipt

Ⓐ This dialog box appears when the sender requests a read receipt.

① Click No.

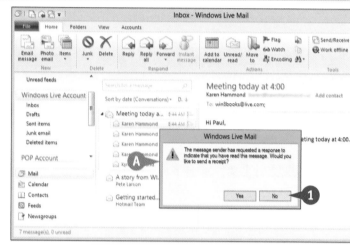

Prevent All Read Receipts

① In Mail, click File.

② Click Options.

③ Click Mail.

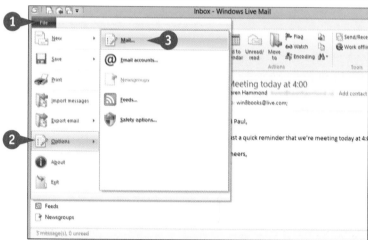

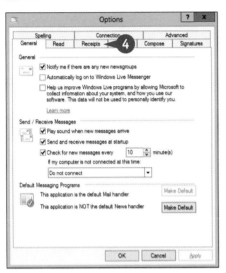

The Options dialog box appears.

4 Click the Receipts tab.

5 Click the Never Send a Read Receipt option (○ changes to ●).

6 Click OK.

Mail stops sending read receipts to confirm that you have read e-mail.

TIPS

More Options!
You may find that read receipts are useful in business. For example, if someone sends you an important message, it is easier to confirm that you have received the message by having Mail send a read receipt than sending a response yourself. In that case, click the Notify Me for Each Read Receipt Request option (○ changes to ●). This enables you to control when you send a read receipt.

More Options!
If you do not mind that other people know when you read a message, you may not want to be bothered with the read receipt dialog box each time a request comes in. In that case, click the Always Send a Read Receipt option (○ changes to ●).

Chapter 10

Getting More Out of Windows 8 Networking

Most computers today do not operate in isolation. Instead, they are usually connected by one method or another to form a network. If you use your computer in a corporate or small business setting, then your network probably consists of computers wired together through devices such as hubs, switches, and routers. If you use your computer at home, then your network probably consists of computers connected wirelessly through a wireless access point.

Whatever the configuration of your network, it usually takes a bit of extra effort to get the network working smoothly and to ensure that users can access network resources. The tasks in this chapter can help you get the most out of your network. You learn how to view the current network status, repair network problems, change the homegroup password, share folders with other network users and protect those folders with advanced permissions, manually connect to a wireless network, share an Internet connection, and hide a network computer.

You can make sure your network is operating at its most efficient by checking its current status from time to time.

These days, networks are generally quite reliable and you can often go for long periods without any problems. Of course, networks are not perfect, so slowdowns, outages, glitches, and other problems are bound to arise occasionally.

You can anticipate potential problems and gather network information in the event of a problem by viewing the network status. The status first tells you the most basic piece of information you require: whether the computer has a connection to the network. Beyond that, the status also tells you how long the computer has been connected to the network, how fast the network connection is, and, for a wireless network, the strength of the wireless signal.

① Press Windows Logo+W.

The Settings search pane appears.

② Type **network status**.

③ Click View Network Status and Tasks.

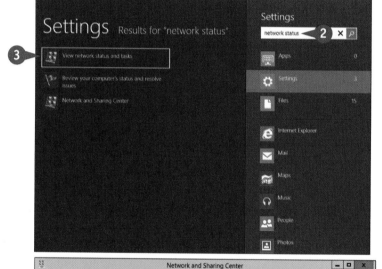

The Network and Sharing Center window appears.

④ Click Change Adapter Settings.

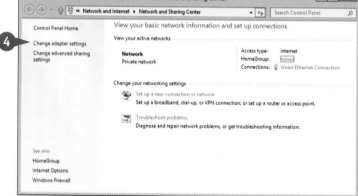

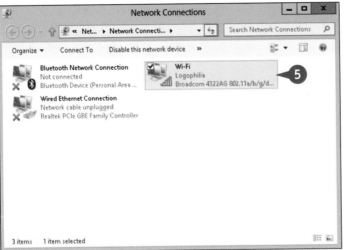

The Network Connections window appears.

5 Double-click the connection you want to check.

The network connection's Status dialog box appears.

Ⓐ The Duration tells you how long this computer has been connected to the network.

Ⓑ The Speed tells you the current network connection speed.

Ⓒ The Signal Quality tells you the strength of the wireless signal (the more green bars you see, the stronger the connection).

6 Click Close.

TIPS

Try This

When you bring your Windows 8 PC or tablet onto an airplane, you must put it into a special state called Airplane mode. This mode turns off the transceivers — the internal components that transmit and receive wireless signals — for the Wi-Fi feature, as well as for Bluetooth and GPS, if your PC has them. To turn on Airplane mode, press Windows Logo+I, click the Network icon (▥), and then click the Airplane Mode switch to On.

More Options!

You may occasionally need to know your computer's current IP (Internet Protocol) address, which is a unique value that identifies your computer on the network. To see your computer's current IP address, follow steps 1 to 5 to display the network connection's Status dialog box. Click Details to display the Network Connection Details dialog box, and then read the IPv4 Address value. Click Close.

Run the Network Diagnostics Tool to Repair Problems

If you have trouble connecting to or accessing your network, Windows 8 comes with a diagnostics tool that can examine your network and then offer solutions.

Networking in Windows 8 usually works quite well right out of the box. That is, you connect your computer to a wired or wireless network, and you can usually see other computers and work with their shared resources right away without the need for a complex configuration procedure.

However, despite the simple networking interface that Windows 8 presents to you, networks are complex structures with many different hardware and software components working together. If just one of those components stops working or becomes unstable, you may encounter network problems. For example, you may no longer be able to log on to a network, you might not see other network computers, or you might not be able to access shared network resources.

When network problems occur, tracking down and solving them is often quite difficult. Fortunately, Windows 8 comes with a tool called Windows Network Diagnostics that automates the process. It analyzes many different aspects of your network setup, and then offers solutions you can try.

① Press Windows Logo+W.

The Settings search pane appears.

② Type **network trouble**.

③ Click Identify and Repair Network Problems.

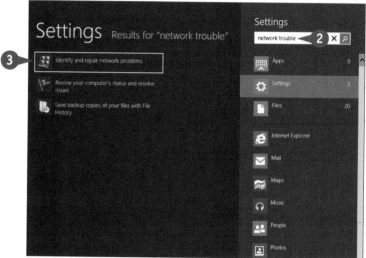

The Windows Network Diagnostics dialog box appears.

④ Implement the solution suggested by Network Diagnostics.

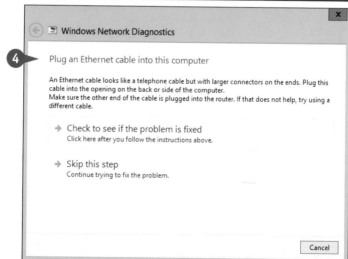

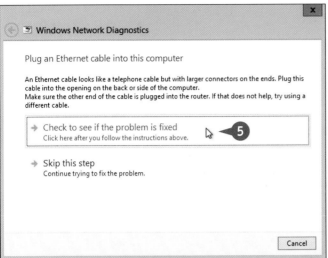

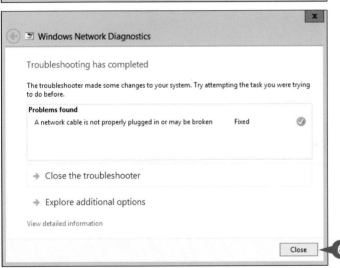

⑤ Click the Check to See If the Problem Is Fixed link.

Windows Network Diagnostics tests your network connection.

If Windows Network Diagnostics finds further problems, repeat steps 3 to 5 as necessary.

The Troubleshooting Has Completed dialog box appears.

⑥ Click Close.

TIPS

More Options!
If you have multiple network adapters in your computer, you may need to test your network connections separately. Press Windows Logo+W, type **connections**, and then click View Network Connections. Right-click the connection you want to test, and then click Diagnose to start Windows Network Diagnostics on that connection.

Try This!
If you have multiple network adapters in your computer, you can often solve a networking problem by disabling all but one of the connections. Press Windows Logo+W, type **connections**, and then click View Network Connections. For each connection you want to disable, right-click the connection and then click Disable.

Display a Network Folder as a Disk Drive

You can gain easier access to a shared network folder by displaying the folder as though it were a disk drive on your computer.

You can use the File Explorer Network folder (click File Explorer and then click Network in the Navigation pane) to view the computers that are part of your network workgroup. If you want to work with a shared folder on one of these computers, you must open the computer that contains the folder, and then open the folder. If you want to work with a subfolder, you must also drill down through the subfolders until you get the one you want.

This is not a big problem if you rarely access network shares. However, navigating a number of folders every time you want to work with a shared resource is inefficient and time-consuming. To save time, Windows 8 enables you to display any shared network folder as though it were a disk drive on your computer. This is called *mapping* the network folder. The advantage of mapping is that an icon for the mapped folder appears in the File Explorer Computer folder (click Computer in the Navigation pane), so you can double-click the icon to access the folder.

---

① In File Explorer, click Computer.

② Click the Computer tab.

③ Click the top half of the Map Network Drive button.

The Map Network Drive dialog box appears.

④ Use the Drive list to click the drive letter you want to use for the mapped network folder.

⑤ Type the address of the shared network folder.

Ⓐ If you are not sure of the address, click Browse, use the Browse for Folder dialog box to click the network folder, and then click OK.

⑥ Click Finish.

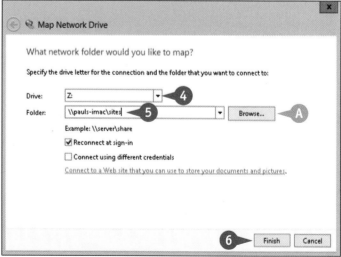

242

If the network share requires credentials different from your own, the Windows Security dialog box appears.

7 Type the username.

8 Type the password.

9 Click Remember My Credentials (☐ changes to ☑).

10 Click OK.

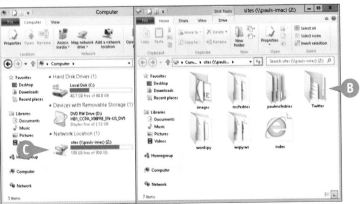

B Windows 8 opens a new window to display the contents of the mapped folder.

C An icon for the mapped folder appears in the Network Location section of the Computer window.

TIPS

Caution!

If you use a removable drive such as a USB flash drive or memory card, Windows 8 automatically assigns a drive letter to this drive. This often causes a conflict if you have a mapped network folder that uses a lower drive letter (such as D, E, or F). Therefore, using higher drive letters (such as X, Y, and Z) for your mapped network folders is good practice.

Remove It!

To speed up the Windows 8 startup and reduce clutter in the Computer window, you can disconnect mapped network folders that you no longer use. Use File Explorer to open the Computer folder, click the Computer tab, click the bottom half of the Map Network Drive button, and then click Disconnect Network Drive. In the Disconnect Network Drives dialog box, click the network drive you want to disconnect, and then click OK.

You can make your Windows 8 homegroup more secure by regularly changing the password.

In a traditional network, file sharing is accomplished via user accounts. If you have just a single user account on a computer, you configure that account's permissions for each shared resource, and you then provide other network users with the username and password. A more likely scenario is to add a user account for each network user, and then configure permissions on shared resources for each of those accounts. This type of file sharing is time-consuming at best and, for new users, dauntingly complex at worst.

With the Windows 8 homegroup feature, access to shared resources is governed by a single password. You set up the homegroup using one Windows 8 computer, and you then share the password among the other Windows 8 computers on the network.

This is much easier, but the password is crucial for network security. To ensure the network remains secure, you should change the homegroup password regularly.

① Press Windows Logo+W.

The Settings search pane appears.

② Type **change homegroup**.

③ Click Change Homegroup Password.

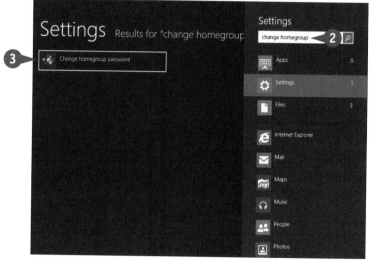

The HomeGroup window appears.

④ Click Change the Password.

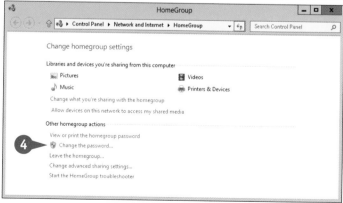

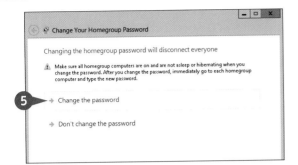

The Change Your Homegroup Password window appears.

5 Click Change the Password.

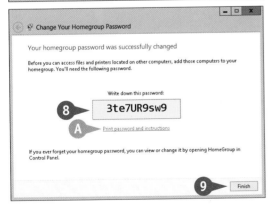

The Type a New Password for Your Homegroup screen appears.

6 Type the password you want to use.

Note: If you prefer to use the password that Windows 8 generates, you can skip this step.

7 Click Next.

The Your Homegroup Password Was Successfully Changed screen appears.

8 Make a note of the new password.

A You can also click this link to print the password.

9 Click Finish.

TIPS

Apply It!
To enter the new password in another homegroup computer, log on to that computer and then follow steps 1 to 3 to open the HomeGroup window. Click Change the Password to open the Update Your Homegroup Password dialog box. Type the new password, click Next, and then click Finish.

View It!
If you forget the homegroup password, follow steps 1 to 3 to open the HomeGroup window, and then click View or Print the Homegroup Password. Windows 8 opens the View and Print Your Homegroup Password window, which displays the homegroup password.

Configure a PC for a Remote Desktop Connection

You can enable other PCs on your network to access a computer's desktop by configuring that computer to accept remote desktop connections.

A remote desktop connection means that your computer connects to a remote computer on your network, and once that connection is made, the remote computer's desktop appears on your computer. You can then use the remote computer as though you were physically sitting down in front of it, including running apps, adjusting

settings, working with files, and customizing Windows 8.

The Windows 8 Remote Desktop feature enables you to connect to a computer's desktop over the network. For this feature to work, the remote PC must be configured to accept remote connections. You must also know the username and password of a user account on the remote PC.

---

① On the computer to which you want to allow remote access, press Windows Logo+W.

The Settings search pane appears.

② Type **remote**.

③ Click Allow Remote Access to Your Computer.

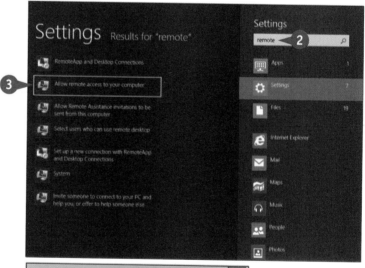

The System Properties dialog box appears with the Remote tab displayed.

④ Click Allow Connections Only from Computers Running Remote Desktop with Network Level Authentication (○ changes to ●).

Note: If you see a message that your computer is set up to sleep or hibernate, click OK.

Note: If you will be connecting to the PC using its administrator account, you can skip to step 10.

⑤ Click Select Users.

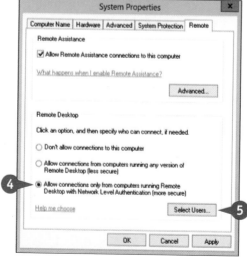

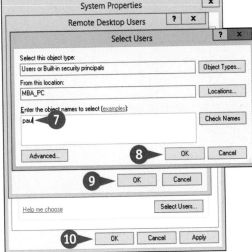

The Remote Desktop Users dialog box appears.

6 Click Add.

The Select Users dialog box appears.

7 Type the name of the user account you want to use to access the PC.

8 Click OK.

9 Click OK.

10 Click OK.

TIPS

Important!
The Allow Connections Only from Computers Running Remote Desktop with Network Level Authentication option is the most secure form of remote desktop access. In this case, Windows 8 checks the connecting PC to see whether its version of Remote Desktop supports Network Level Authentication (NLA). NLA is a security protocol that authenticates the user before making the remote desktop connection. NLA is built in to every version of Windows 8, 7, and Vista, but is not supported on older Windows systems.

Did You Know?
Not all versions of Windows 8 can accept remote desktop connections. In fact, only Windows 8 Pro can act as a remote desktop host. If your computer is running Windows 8 or Windows 8 RT, it cannot be used for remote desktop connections.

Connect to a Remote PC's Desktop

You can take advantage of the apps and data that reside on a remote network PC by connecting to that PC's desktop.

You probably share a folder or two on your computer, and it is likely that other people on your network are similarly generous with some of their folders. Sharing folders is an easy way to give and get access to other users' files, but it does not solve all the sharing problems you might come across. For example, you cannot share programs, and you cannot share data such as e-mail messages.

To solve these and similar problems, you need to go beyond shared folders and establish a more powerful connection to the remote computer. That is, you need to connect to the remote machine's desktop, which enables you to open folders, run programs, edit documents, and adjust settings. In short, anything you can do while physically sitting in front of the other computer you can do remotely from your own computer.

Connect to the Remote Desktop

① Click Desktop.

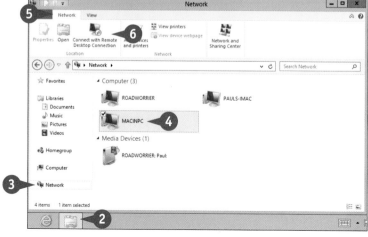

The Desktop app appears.

② Click File Explorer.

③ Click Network.

④ Click the remote PC.

⑤ Click the Network tab.

⑥ Click Connect with Remote Desktop Connection.

Remote Desktop prompts you to log on to the remote PC.

⑦ Type or click the username for an account on the remote PC.

⑧ Type the account password.

⑨ Click Remember My Credentials (☐ changes to ☑).

⑩ Click OK.

Note: *If you see a dialog box waning you that the identity of the remote computer cannot be verified, click Yes.*

The remote PC's screen appears.

Work with the Remote PC

ⓐ Remote Desktop Connection displays the connection bar for the remote PC.

ⓑ Click Show the Commands for the Remote PC to display a list of commands for working with the remote PC.

ⓒ Click Unpin the Connection Bar to hide the connection bar.

Note: *To display a hidden connection bar, move the mouse pointer to the top of the screen.*

① To launch an app, click its tile.

② Click Close to close the connection.

TIP

More Options

To work with apps on the remote PC, click Show the Commands for the Remote PC to display the list of commands. You have the following options:

● Click App Commands to see the application bar for the current remote app.
● Click Charms to display the remote PC's Charms menu.
● Click Snap to snap the current app on the remote PC.
● Click Switch Apps to switch from one app to another on the remote PC.
● Click Start to return to the remote PC's Start screen.

Share a Folder with Other Users on the Network

You can collaborate with other people on your network and allow users to work with some of your documents by sharing a folder with the network.

The purpose of most networks is to share resources between the computers connected to the network. For example, the users on a network can share a single printer or an Internet connection.

This resource sharing also applies to documents. It might be a presentation that you want other people to comment on, a database with information that you want others to use, or a

worksheet that you want people to modify. In all these cases, the easiest way to give other people access to your documents is to share the document folder with the network. This section shows you how to set up basic folder sharing. See the next section to learn how to protect your shared folders with permissions.

To follow the steps in this section, you need to deactivate the Windows 8 Sharing Wizard. In Chapter 3, see the section "Switch to Advanced Sharing to Improve Security" to learn how to deactivate this wizard.

---

1 Open the folder that contains the folder you want to share.

2 Click the folder you want to share.

3 Click the Share tab.

4 Click Advanced Sharing.

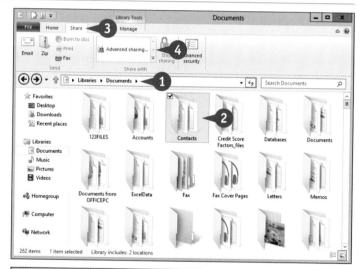

The folder's Properties dialog box appears.

5 Click Advanced Sharing.

The Advanced Sharing dialog box appears.

6 Click the Share This Folder check box (☐ changes to ☑).

7 Edit the Share Name, if desired.

8 Click OK.

9 Click Close.

Windows 8 begins sharing the folder.

More Options!

If you want to change the share name of your folder, first follow steps 1 to 5 to display the Advanced Sharing dialog box. Click Add to display the New Share dialog box, type the new share name you want to use, and then click OK. Use the Share Name list to click the old share name and then click Remove. Click OK and then click Close.

Reverse It!

If you no longer want network users to access a folder, you can stop sharing it. Follow steps 1 to 5 to open the Advanced Sharing dialog box. Click the Share This Folder check box (☑ changes to ☐). Click OK and then click Close.

Protect Your Shared Files with Advanced File Permissions

You can use file permissions to specify which network users can access which folders, and what exactly those users can do with the files in those folders.

Chapter 3 discussed using file permissions to control what other users on your computer can do with your files. Windows 8 offers a similar set of permissions for folders that you have shared with the network. Permissions designate exactly what specified users can do with the contents of the protected network folder. In this case, there are three types of permissions.

With *Full Control* permission, network users can view and modify the shared resource, as well as change permissions on the resource. With *Change* permission, network users can view the folder contents, open files, edit files, create new files and subfolders, delete files, and run programs. With *Read* permission, network users can open files but cannot edit them.

In each case, you can either allow the permission or deny it.

① Follow steps 1 to 5 in the previous section to open the Advanced Sharing dialog box.

② Click Permissions.

The folder's Permissions dialog box appears.

③ Click Add.

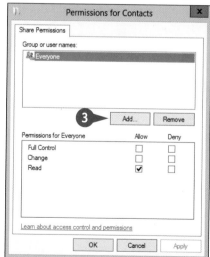

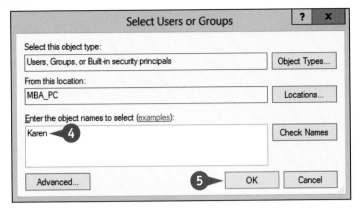

The Select Users or Groups dialog box appears.

④ Type the name of the user you want to work with.

⑤ Click OK.

Ⓐ The user appears in this list.

⑥ Click the new user to select it.

⑦ In the Allow column, click each permission that you want to allow (☐ changes to ☑).

⑧ Click OK.

⑨ Click OK in the Advanced Sharing dialog box.

⑩ Click Close in the folder's Properties dialog box.

Windows protects the folder with the permissions you selected.

TIPS

Caution!
By default, Windows 8 assigns Read permission to the Everyone group. This group represents every user or group not otherwise specified in the Permissions dialog box. For extra security, make sure you do not give the Everyone group Full Control or Change permission. If you want only your specified users and groups to access your shared folder, follow steps 1 and 2, click Everyone, and then click Remove.

More Options!
You can save time when setting up shared folder security by assigning permissions to groups instead of individual users. For example, if you know that some of the network users have administrator accounts, you could add the Administrators group; similarly, all standard Windows 8 users are part of the Users group. Follow the same steps, but when you get to step 4, type the name of the group instead of the name of a user.

Manually Connect to a Hidden Wireless Network

If a nearby wireless network is not broadcasting its identity, you can still connect to that network by entering the connection settings manually.

Each wireless network has a network name — often called the Service Set Identifier, or SSID — that identifies the network to wireless devices and computers with wireless network cards. By default, most wireless networks broadcast the network name so that you can see the network and connect to it. However, some wireless networks disable network name broadcasting as a security precaution. The reasoning here is that if an unauthorized user cannot see the network, he or she cannot attempt to connect to it. (However, some devices can pick up the network name when authorized computers connect to the network, so this is not a foolproof security measure.)

You can still connect to a hidden wireless network by entering the connection settings manually. You need to know the network name, the network's security type and encryption type, and the network's security key or passphrase.

① Press Windows Logo+W.

The Settings search pane appears.

② Type **connection**.

③ Click Set Up a Connection or Network.

The Choose a Connection Option window appears.

④ Click Manually Connect to a Wireless Network.

⑤ Click Next.

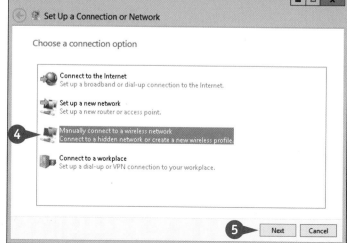

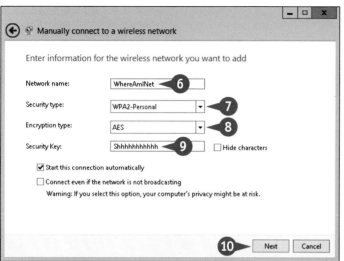

6 Type the network name.

7 Use the Security Type list to click the network's security type.

8 Use the Encryption Type list to click the network's encryption type (if any).

9 Type the network's security key.

10 Click Next.

Windows 8 adds the network to the list of available wireless networks.

11 Click Close.

Apply It!

Windows 8 does not connect you to the hidden wireless network automatically. The steps you followed in this section only add the network to the list of available wireless networks. To make the connection, press Windows Logo+I to open the Settings pane, click the Network icon (⚃), click the wireless network, and then click Connect. If Windows 8 prompts you for the security key, type the key and click OK.

More Options!

By default, Windows 8 activates the Connect Automatically check box. This saves you from having to repeat the steps in this section each time you want to connect to the network. However, Windows 8 may not connect automatically if the network is not broadcasting. To work around this, click the Connect Even if the Network Is Not Broadcasting check box (☐ changes to ☑) after step 9.

Share an Internet Connection

You can save time and maintain network security by giving non-network computers indirect access to your network's Internet connection.

One of the key benefits of setting up a network is to share a single Internet connection. This is almost always done by connecting the Internet provider's modem to a network router, using the router to connect to the Internet, and then giving Internet access to every computer that connects to the router.

However, you might come across a situation where you want to give a computer access to the Internet, but you do not want to connect that

computer to your network. For example, you might have a visitor who needs to use the Internet temporarily. In this case, you probably do not want to take the time to get that person on your network, and you might not want to expose your network to the person.

Whatever the reason, you can use Internet Connection Sharing (ICS) to share a computer's existing Internet connection with other users. This means that you can connect the guest PC to that computer using a network cable, and the guest PC immediately gets Internet access without full network access.

① On the computer you want to use for ICS, press Windows Logo+W.

The Settings search pane appears.

② Type **view connections**.

③ Click View Network Connections.

The Network Connections window appears.

④ Right-click the connection you use for Internet access.

⑤ Click Properties.

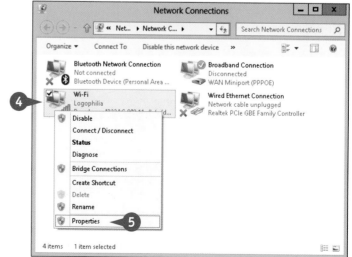

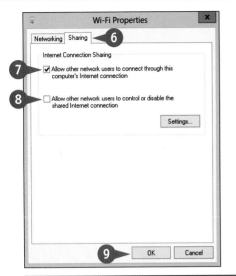

The connection's Properties dialog box appears.

6 Click the Sharing tab.

7 Click Allow Other Network Users to Connect Through This Computer's Internet Connection (☐ changes to ☑).

8 Click Allow Other Network Users to Control or Disable the Shared Internet Connection (☑ changes to ☐).

9 Click OK.

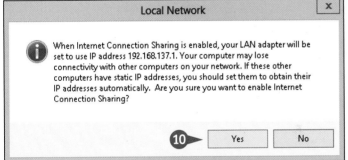

Windows 8 asks you to confirm.

10 Click Yes.

Windows 8 begins sharing the computer's Internet connection.

Did You Know?

You can also share a direct broadband or dial-up connection. However, for this to work, you must set up the connection to allow other people to use it. When you create the connection, click Allow Other People to Use This Connection (☐ changes to ☑).

Important!

For the guest PC to use the host computer's shared Internet connection, that PC must be configured to get its Internet configuration data automatically. This is usually the default configuration, but you should check just to be sure. On the guest PC, follow steps 1 to 3 to open the Network Connections window, right-click the Ethernet connection, click Properties, and double-click Internet Protocol Version 4. Click Obtain an IP Address Automatically (○ changes to ◉), click Obtain DNS Server Address Automatically (○ changes to ◉), and then click OK.

Hide a Computer on the Network

If you have a computer that you do not want other network users to see, you can hide that computer on your network.

One of the main reasons to create a local network is to enable users from multiple computers to share and use each other's resources, such as documents, media files and devices, hard drives, and printers. If you do not want other network users to work with the resources of a particular computer, the simplest way to go about this is to not share any resources on that PC. However, other users can still see the PC in the Network window, and all

Windows PCs share several hidden resources by default.

The only way to avoid any user from accessing a network PC's resources is to hide that PC from the rest of the network. Note, however, that after you do this, the hidden PC will also not be able to see other computers on the network, and so will not be able to access the shared resources on those PCs. The exceptions are mapped network drives, which the hidden PC will still be able to use normally, provided the mappings were performed before hiding the PC.

① Press Windows Logo+W.

The Settings search pane appears.

② Type **sharing center**.

③ Click Network and Sharing Center.

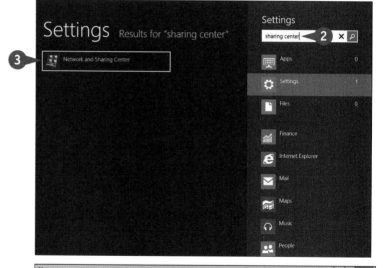

The Network and Sharing Center window appears.

④ Click Change Advanced Sharing Settings.

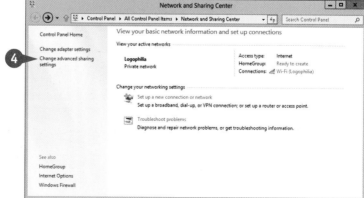

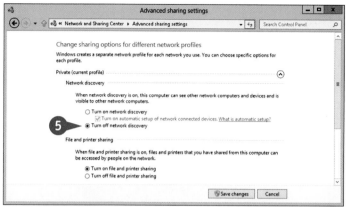

The Advanced Sharing Settings window appears.

⑤ Click Turn Off Network Discovery (○ changes to ◉).

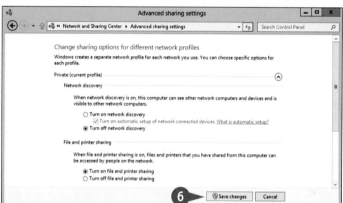

⑥ Click Save Changes.

More Options!

If you use your PC on public networks such as wireless hotspots, you should make sure you have your PC hidden on those networks. Windows 8 does this by default, but it does not hurt to check. When connected to a public network, follow steps 1 to 4, open the Guest or Public profile, and then click Turn Off Network Discovery (○ changes to ◉).

Reverse It!

If you want to have your computer visible on the network later on, you can turn network discovery back on. One way to do this is to follow steps 1 to 4 and then click Turn On Network Discovery (○ changes to ◉). Alternatively, run File Explorer and click Network. When you see the Information bar that says "Network discovery is turned off," click the bar and then click Turn On Network Discovery and File Sharing.

Maximizing PC Maintenance

Computer problems, like the proverbial death and taxes, seem to be one of those constants in life. Whether it is a hard disk failure, a power outage that destroys some files, or a virus that invades your system, the issue is not *whether* something will go wrong, but rather *when* it will happen. Instead of waiting to deal with these difficulties after they have occurred, you need to become proactive and perform maintenance on your system in advance. This not only reduces the chances that something will go wrong, but it also sets up your system to recover more easily from any problems that do occur.

This chapter shows you various Windows 8 settings, tools, and techniques that can help you do just that. You learn how to schedule maintenance and defragmentation, how to delete unneeded files, how to reset your computer, and how to safeguard your PC with a recovery drive, a system image backup, and restore points. You also learn how to recover from problems by reverting to an earlier restore point, and how to access the Windows 8 recovery tools.

Schedule Automatic Maintenance

You can make Windows 8 automatic maintenance chores more convenient by changing the time when they are scheduled to occur.

When you set up Windows 8, you were asked to choose how you wanted to handle the periodic updates that Microsoft makes available for bug fixes, security enhancements, and updated features. If you chose the option to have the updates installed automatically, then Windows 8 automatically checks for, downloads, and installs updates during the *maintenance window*, which is defined by default as follows:

- Maintenance is performed each day at 3:00 a.m.
- If you are using your computer, maintenance is postponed until you are no longer using it.

- If your computer is in sleep mode, maintenance is postponed until the computer is awake.
- If the maintenance server is running late, maintenance is postponed until the server is ready, as long as your computer is not being used and is awake.

Windows 8 uses the maintenance window not only to check for updates, but also to run Windows Defender security scans and to perform system diagnostics. If the default 3:00 a.m. window is inconvenient for you, you can configure the maintenance window to a time more suited to your own schedule.

---

1 Press Windows Logo+W.

The Settings search pane appears.

2 Type **maintenance**.

3 Click Change Automatic Maintenance Settings.

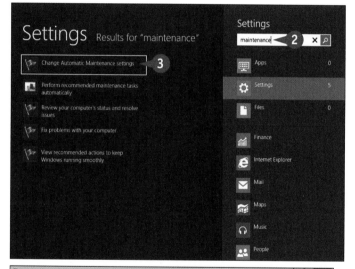

The Automatic Maintenance window appears.

4 Click the Run Maintenance Tasks Daily At ▾.

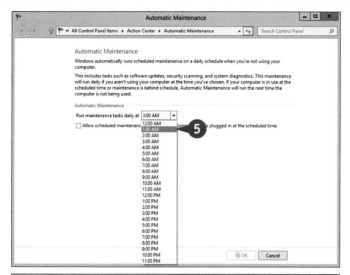

5 Click the time you want to use as the basis of the maintenance window.

6 Click OK.

Windows 8 uses the new time as the start of the maintenance window.

Change the Defragmentation Schedule

If you want to defragment your hard disk either more often or less often, you can change the default schedule.

Windows 8 comes with a utility called Disk Defragmenter that is an essential tool for tuning your hard disk. This utility's job is to rid your hard disk of file fragmentation.

File fragmentation means that a file is stored on your hard disk in scattered, noncontiguous bits. This is a performance drag because it means that when Windows 8 tries to open a file, it must make several stops to collect the various pieces. If a lot of files are fragmented, it can slow even the fastest hard disk to a crawl.

That is why, by default, Windows 8 automatically defragments all of your system's hard drives once a week during the system maintenance window (see the previous section).

If you use your computer frequently and are constantly installing and uninstalling programs and creating and working with large data files, then you might see a performance boost if you configured Windows 8 to defragment your hard drives daily. If you do not use your computer very often, or if you only work with small files, then you can probably get away with a monthly defragmentation.

---

1 Press Windows Logo+W.

The Settings search pane appears.

2 Type **defrag**.

3 Click Defragment and Optimize Your Drives.

The Optimize Drives window appears.

4 Click Change Settings.

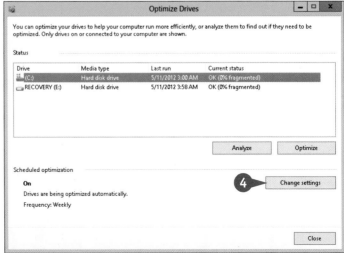

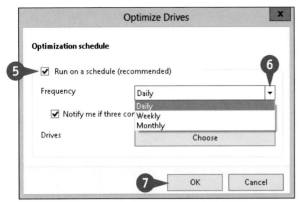

The Optimization Schedule settings appear.

⑤ Make sure Run on a Schedule is checked (☐ changes to ☑).

⑥ Click the Frequency ⏷ and then click the defragmentation frequency you want to use: Daily, Weekly, or Monthly.

⑦ Click OK.

⑧ Click Close.

Windows 8 applies the new defragmentation schedule.

TIP

Try This!

There are some situations where it is worthwhile to augment the Windows 8 automatic defragment operations with some manual defragments. For example, before you install a large program, it would be useful to defragment the installation drive to give the program the best chance of installing its files contiguously. Also, you can often improve your PC's performance by defragmenting a hard drive twice in a row.

To run a defragment manually, follow steps 1 to 3 to open the Optimize Drives window. Click the drive you want to defragment and then click Optimize. Note that you will most often want to defragment the Windows drive. This is usually C, but look for the drive with the Windows logo.

Free Up Disk Space by Deleting Unneeded Files

To free up hard drive space on your computer and keep Windows 8 running efficiently, you can use the Disk Cleanup program to delete files that your system no longer needs.

Today's hard drives are quite large, with capacities measured in the hundreds or even thousands of gigabytes. However, the expanding capacity of modern hard drives has been offset to a certain extent by the expanding amount of data that we store on those drives. This is partially due to the increasing size of many software programs. However, it is mostly caused by extremely large media files (such as digital

movies and TV shows) and extremely large collections of smaller media files (particularly digital music and photos), all of which can take up a lot of space on a hard drive. This means that even with hard drive capacities measured in terabytes (thousands of gigabytes), it is still possible to run low on storage space.

Therefore, you should run Disk Cleanup whenever your hard drive free space becomes too low, particularly less than about 25GB. If hard drive space is not a problem, you should still run Disk Cleanup every two or three months.

1. Press Windows Logo+W.

    The Settings search pane appears.

2. Type **disk cleanup**.

3. Click Free Up Disk Space by Deleting Unnecessary Files.

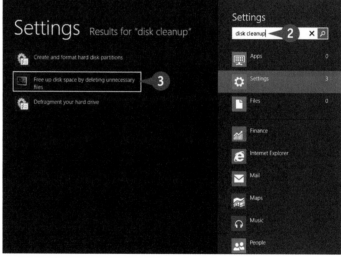

If your computer has more than one drive, the Drive Selection dialog box appears.

4. Click the Drives ▾ and then click the hard drive you want to clean up.

5. Click OK.

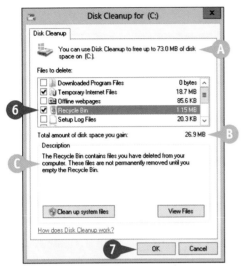

After a few moments, the Disk Cleanup dialog box appears.

Ⓐ This area displays the total amount of drive space you can free up.

Ⓑ This area displays the amount of drive space the activated options will free up.

⑥ Click the check box (☐ changes to ☑) for each file type that you want to delete.

Ⓒ This area displays a description of the highlighted file type.

⑦ Click OK.

Disk Cleanup asks you to confirm that you want to delete the file types.

⑧ Click Delete Files.

TIPS

Did You Know?
Here are the main types of files that Disk Cleanup can remove from your system:

- **Downloaded Program files**: Small web page programs downloaded onto your hard drive.
- **Temporary Internet files**: Web page copies stored on your hard drive for faster viewing.
- **Offline webpages**: Web page copies stored on your hard drive for offline viewing.
- **Recycle Bin**: Files that you have deleted since you last emptied your Recycle Bin.
- **Temporary files**: Files used by programs to store temporary data.
- **Thumbnails**: Miniature versions of images and other content used in folder windows.

More Options!
You can free up even more disk space by clicking the Clean Up System Files button. This enables you to remove files that Windows no longer needs.

Reset Your Computer

If you find that your computer is running extremely slowly or that Windows 8 or your programs are constantly freezing or crashing, you can get a fresh start by resetting your computer.

In Chapter 6, you learned how to refresh your PC's system files, and that procedure should solve most problems. If for some reason it does not, or if you do not have enough room on your hard drive to perform the refresh, then your next option is to completely reset your PC. The Reset Your PC feature completely erases your data, formats your hard drive, and then reinstalls Windows 8, so it is a fairly drastic step. If

possible, you should back up your files before resetting your computer.

Reset Your PC is also useful if you are donating or selling your PC. You probably do not want the recipient to be able to see your documents, media files, e-mail messages, Internet Explorer favorites, and other personal data. Rather than deleting this data manually, Reset Your PC overwrites your information with random data, so the recipient cannot see it.

How you use Reset Your PC depends on whether you can still access Windows 8 or whether you need to use a recovery drive.

Reset Your PC from Windows 8

1 Press Windows Logo+I.

The Settings search appears.

2 Click Change PC Settings.

The PC Settings app runs.

3 Click the General tab.

4 Click Get Started.

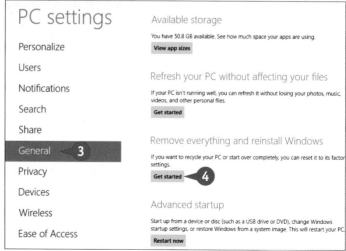

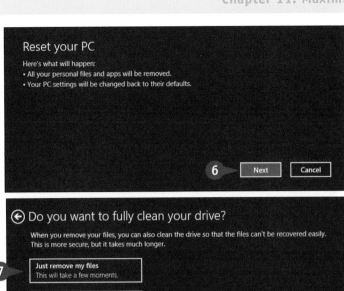

Reset Your PC explains the process.

⑤ Insert your Windows 8 installation disc or a Windows 8 recovery drive.

⑥ Click Next.

Note: *If you see a message about removing files from all drives, click Only the Drive Where Windows Is Installed.*

Reset Your PC asks how you want to remove your personal files.

⑦ Click the process you prefer.

Note: *See the first tip in this section to learn more about the two removal options.*

⑧ Click Reset.

Windows 8 resets your computer.

TIP

Did You Know?
When it comes to removing your personal files, Reset Your PC offers two options: Just Remove My Files and Fully Clean the Drive. The Just Remove My Files option deletes your data in the sense that after Windows is reset, it can no longer work with or see the data. However, the data remains on the PC's hard drive, so a person with special tools can access the data. The Full Clean the Drive option prevents this by overwriting your information with random data, which can take quite a bit of time, but is much more secure.

continued ▶

If you cannot start Windows 8 because of a problem, you can still run Reset Your PC from a Windows 8 recovery drive.

Some Windows problems are so severe that they prevent you from even starting your system. However, Windows 8 enables you to start your PC from another drive. In particular, you can start your PC using a Windows 8 recovery drive, which is a USB flash drive that contains special files that can help you recover your system. You can

learn how to create a USB recovery drive in the next section.

Once you start from the recovery drive, you enter the *recovery environment*, a special set of tools that help you recover from problems. One of these tools is Reset Your PC, which wipes your system and installs a fresh copy of Windows 8, which should fix the problem and get your system back on its feet.

Refresh Your PC from a Recovery Drive

1 Insert the recovery drive.

2 Restart your PC.

3 Boot to the recovery drive.

Note: *How you boot to the USB drive depends on your system.*

Ⓐ In some cases, you see a message telling you to press a key.

Ⓑ In some cases, you select a boot device from a menu.

The Windows 8 recovery environment appears.

Note: *If you see the Choose Your Keyboard Layout screen, click US.*

4 Click Troubleshoot.

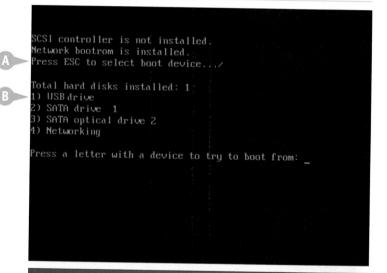

```
SCSI controller is not installed.
Network bootrom is installed.
Press ESC to select boot device.../

Total hard disks installed: 1
1) USB drive
2) SATA drive  1
3) SATA optical drive 2
4) Networking

Press a letter with a device to try to boot from: _
```

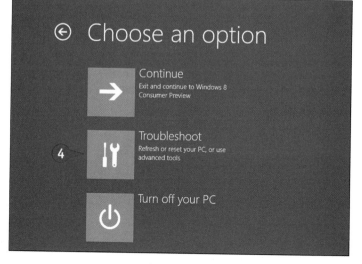

← **Choose an option**

Continue
Exit and continue to Windows 8 Consumer Preview

Troubleshoot
Refresh or reset your PC, or use advanced tools

Turn off your PC

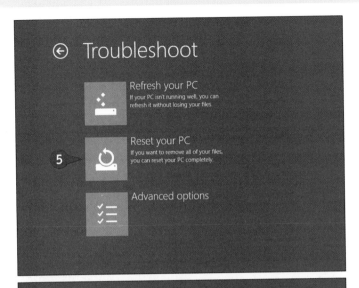

The Troubleshoot screen appears.

5 Click Reset Your PC.

Reset Your PC explains the process.

6 Click Next.

7 Follow steps 7 and 8 in the first set of steps.

Windows 8 resets your computer.

TIP

More Options!
If you do not have a Windows 8 recovery drive, you can also run Reset Your PC from your Windows installation media. Insert the media, restart your computer, and then boot to the media drive. When the Windows Setup dialog box appears, click Next, click Repair Your Computer, and then follow steps 4 to 7.

Create a USB Recovery Drive

You can make it easier to troubleshoot and recover from computer problems by creating a USB recovery drive.

We all hope our computers operate trouble-free over their lifetimes, but we know from bitter experience that this is rarely the case. Computers are incredibly complex systems, so it is almost inevitable that a PC will develop glitches. If your hard drive is still accessible, you can boot to Windows 8 and access the recovery tools, as described later in this chapter.

If you cannot boot your PC, however, then you must boot using some other drive. If you have your Windows 8 installation media, you can boot using that drive. If you do not have the installation media, you can still recover if you have created a USB recovery drive. This is a USB flash drive that contains the Windows 8 recovery environment, which enables you to refresh or reset your PC, use System Restore, recover a system image, and more.

① Insert the USB flash drive you want to use.

② Press Windows Logo+W.

③ Type **recovery drive**.

④ Click Create a Recovery Drive.

The User Account Control dialog box appears.

⑤ Click Yes.

Note: *If you are using a standard account, enter your PC's administrator credentials to continue.*

The Recovery Drive Wizard appears.

⑥ Click Next.

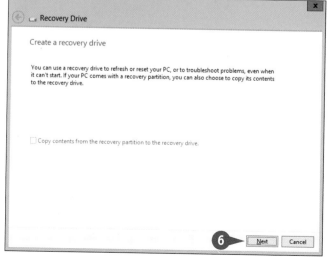

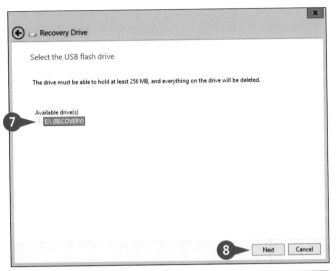

The Recovery Drive Wizard prompts you to choose the USB flash drive.

⑦ Click the drive, if it is not selected already.

⑧ Click Next.

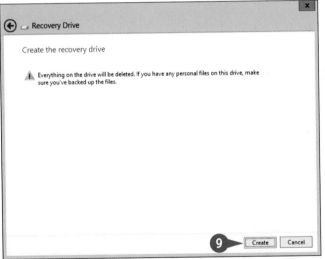

The Recovery Drive Wizard warns you that all the data on the drive will be deleted.

⑨ Click Create.

The wizard formats the drive and copies the recovery tools and data.

⑩ Click Finish (not shown).

TIPS

Did You Know?

To use a USB flash drive as a recovery drive, the drive must have a capacity of at least 256MB. Also, Windows 8 will erase all data on the drive, so make sure the flash drive does not contain any files you want to keep. If it does, be sure to move those files to a different drive before you begin this procedure.

Test It!

To make sure your recovery drive works properly, you should test it by booting your PC to the drive. Insert the recovery drive and then restart your PC. How you boot to the drive depends on your system. Some PCs display a menu of boot devices, and you select the USB drive from that menu. In other cases, you see a message telling you to press a key.

Safeguard Your Computer with a System Image Backup

To protect yourself in the event your system hard drive fails or otherwise becomes unusable, you can create a system image backup.

The worst-case scenario for PC problems is a system crash that renders your hard disk or system files unusable. Your only recourse in such a case is to start from scratch with either a reformatted hard disk or a new hard disk. This usually means that you have to reinstall Windows 8 and then reinstall and reconfigure all your applications. In other words, you are looking at

the better part of a day or, more likely, a few days, to recover your system. However, Windows 8 has a feature that takes most of the pain out of recovering your system. It is called a *system image backup* and is actually a complete backup of your Windows 8 installation. It takes a long time to create a system image (at least several hours, depending on how much stuff you have), but it is worth it for the peace of mind it gives you.

---

① Press Windows Logo+W.

The Settings search pane appears.

② Type **file recovery**.

③ Click Windows 7 File Recovery.

The Windows 7 File Recovery window appears.

④ Click Create a System Image.

The Create a System Image Wizard appears.

⑤ Select a backup destination (○ changes to ●):

On a Hard Disk: Select this option to use a disk drive on your computer.

On One or More DVDs: Select this option if you want to use DVDs to hold the backup.

On a Network Location: Select this option if you want to use a shared network folder.

⑥ Click Next.

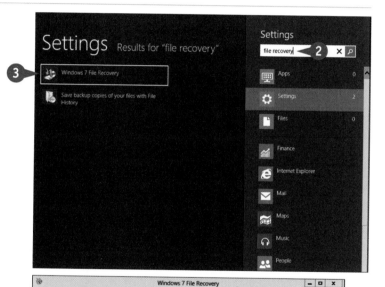

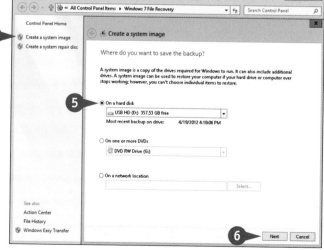

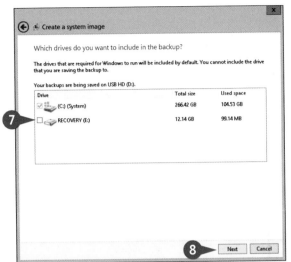

The Which Drives Do You Want to Include in the Backup? screen appears.

7 Select the check box beside each extra drive you want to add to the backup (☐ changes to ☑).

8 Click Next.

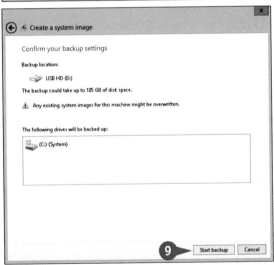

Windows 8 asks you to confirm your backup settings.

9 Click Start Backup.

Windows 8 creates the system image.

More Options!

When the system image backup is complete, Windows 8 asks if you want to create a system repair disc. You do not need a system repair disc if you have already created a USB recovery drive, as described in the previous section, so click No. If you do not have a USB recovery drive and you do not have a USB flash drive to create one, click Yes instead.

Apply It!

If worse comes to worst and you are forced to start over with a formatted or new hard drive, you need to restore the system image. If you have a USB recovery drive, boot to it and then click a keyboard layout; if you have the Windows 8 install media, boot to it, click Next, and then click Repair Your Computer. Click Troubleshoot, click Advanced Options, and then click System Image Recovery.

Create a System Restore Point

If your computer crashes or becomes unstable after you install a program or a new device, the System Restore feature in Windows 8 can fix things by restoring the system to an earlier state. To ensure this works, you need to set restore points before you install programs and devices on your computer.

Windows 8 automatically creates system restore points as follows: every week (called a *system checkpoint*); before installing an update; and before installing certain programs (such as

Microsoft Office) and devices. These are useful, but it pays to err on the side of caution and create your own restore points more often. This is particularly true if you are installing older programs or devices that might not work well with Windows 8 or that are not certified to be compatible with Windows 8. These programs and devices can create system instabilities, so having a restore point to fall back on ensures that you can return your system to a fully functioning state.

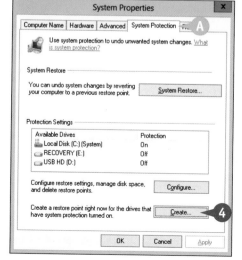

① Press Windows Logo+W.

The Settings search pane appears.

② Type **protection**.

③ Click Create a Restore Point.

The System Properties dialog box appears.

Ⓐ The System Protection tab is already displayed.

④ Click Create.

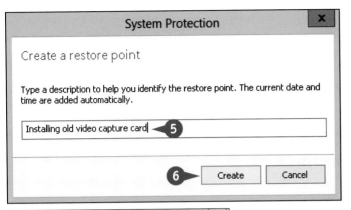

The Create a Restore Point dialog box appears.

5 Type a description for your restore point.

6 Click Create.

System Restore creates the restore point.

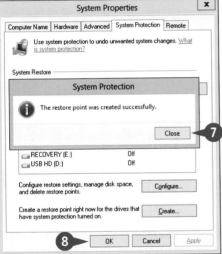

Windows 8 tells you the restore point was created successfully.

7 Click Close.

8 Click OK to close the System Properties dialog box.

More Options!
By default, Windows 8 sets aside between three and five percent of your hard disk space for restore points. When that space is used up, Windows 8 deletes the oldest restore points as new ones are added. If you use restore points frequently and you have a lot of free space on your hard drive, consider increasing the amount of space allotted to restore points. Follow steps 1 to 3 to open the System Properties dialog box, click Configure, and then adjust the Max Usage slider to the percentage value you want to use.

Revert to an Earlier Restore Point

If your computer becomes unstable or behaves erratically after you install a program or device, you can often fix the problem by applying a restore point you created before making the change.

If after you install a program or device you notice problems with your system, the easiest solution is to uninstall the item. If that does not work, then your next step is to revert to an earlier restore point. Windows 8 reverts your computer to the configuration it had when you created the restore point, which should solve the problem.

Note, too, that reverting to an earlier restore point is a useful way to solve a malware problem. If you accidentally allow a virus, Trojan horse, or spyware onto your PC, it is almost impossible to get rid of these programs manually. Anti-malware software is usually the best solution, but some malware blocks the use of these programs. You can almost always get rid of malware by booting to Safe Mode (see the section, "Access the Recovery Tools") and then reverting to a restore point that predates the infection.

---

① Press Windows Logo+W.

The Settings search pane appears.

② Type **protection**.

③ Click Create a Restore Point.

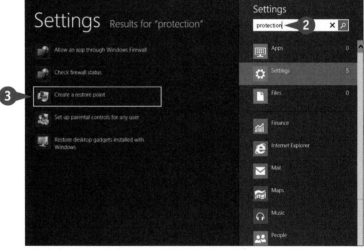

The System Properties dialog box appears.

④ Click System Restore.

The System Restore dialog box appears.

Ⓐ System Restore might show the most likely restore point here. If this is the restore point you want, or if you do not see a restore point, skip to step 8.

⑤ Click Choose a Different Restore Point
(○ changes to ◉).

⑥ Click Next.

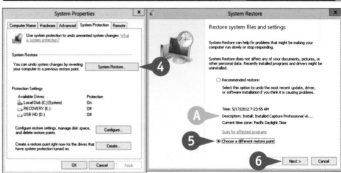

278

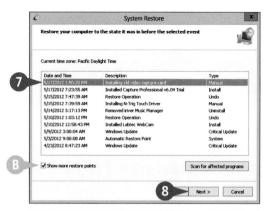

System Restore prompts you to choose a restore point.

⑦ Click the restore point you want to apply.

Ⓑ If you do not see the restore point you want, click Show More Restore Points (☐ changes to ☑).

⑧ Click Next.

The Confirm Your Restore Point dialog box appears.

⑨ Click Finish.

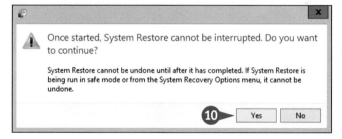

System Restore asks you to confirm that you want to restore your system.

⑩ Click Yes.

System Restore applies the restore point and then restarts Windows 8.

TIPS

Important!

If you are trying to get rid of malware or if Windows 8 will not start properly, you can often solve the problem by booting to Safe Mode (see the next section) and then reverting to a restore point that predates the problem. To run System Restore in Safe Mode, press Windows Logo+X, click Control Panel, click Recovery, click Advanced Tools, and then click Open System Restore.

Remove It!

If applying the restore point makes things worse, you can reverse it. Follow steps 1 to 6 to display the list of available restore points on your computer. Click the Restore Operation restore point, and then follow steps 8 to 10.

If you are having a problem with your computer, you can troubleshoot and hopefully solve the problem by using the Windows 8 recovery tools.

You can perform many troubleshooting tasks from within Windows 8. For example, you can shut down and restart a program, uninstall a program or device, update a device driver, restore a previous version of a file from your history, and so on. Even signing off and then signing in or rebooting your computer will often solve many problems.

However, there are more intractable problems that require you to leave Windows 8 and enter what is known as the *Recovery Environment* (or RE). The RE offers a simple, easily navigated set of screens that give you access to a number of troubleshooting and recovery-related tools and utilities. These tools include Reset Your PC (covered earlier in this chapter) and Refresh Your PC (covered in Chapter 6). This section shows you how to access the Windows 8 Recovery Environment.

① Press Windows Logo+I.

The Settings pane appears.

② Click Change PC Settings.

The PC Settings app appears.

③ Click General.

④ At the bottom of the screen, click Restart Now.

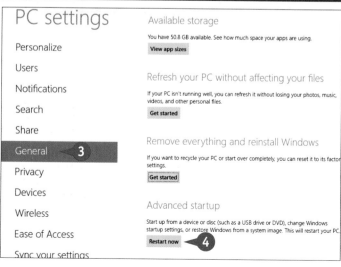

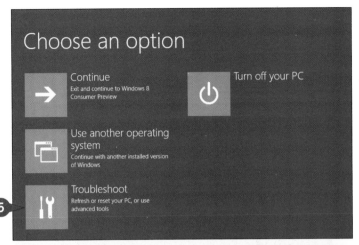

Windows 8 displays the Choose an Option screen.

⑤ Click Troubleshoot.

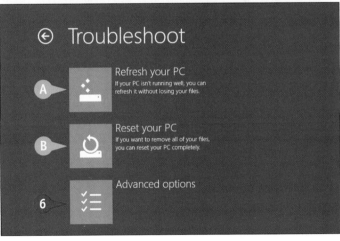

Windows 8 displays the Troubleshoot screen.

Ⓐ Click Refresh Your PC to reinstall Windows 8 without losing your personal files.

Ⓑ Click Reset Your PC to wipe your hard drive and reinstall Windows 8.

⑥ Click Advanced Options.

TIPS

More Options!
If you cannot start Windows 8, you can still access the advanced startup options as long as you have a USB recovery drive or the Windows 8 install media. If you have a USB recovery drive, boot to it and then click a keyboard layout; if you have the Windows 8 install media, boot to it, click Next, and then click Repair Your Computer. Then follow from step 5 onward in this section.

Try This!
In Chapter 1, you learned how to add a shutdown tile to the Start screen. If you access the Recovery Environment frequently, consider adding a tile that automatically boots Windows 8 to the RE. Follow the steps in the "Add a Shutdown Tile to the Start Screen" section in Chapter 1, but when you specify the command to run, type the following:

shutdown.exe /o /r /t 00

continued ▶

The Windows 8 RE includes a number of tools that can help you get your system back on its feet. These tools also include System Restore to revert to an earlier configuration (see "Revert to an Earlier Restore Point," earlier in this chapter) and System Image Recovery to restore your entire configuration from a system image backup (see "Safeguard Your Computer with a System Image Backup," earlier in this chapter).

The Windows 8 RE also includes an Automatic Repair command, which is useful if you are having problems starting Windows 8. Automatic Repair analyzes your system startup and then attempts several repair strategies.

You can also use the RE to run Command Prompt, which enables you to run command-line tools and utilities.

Finally, the RE also gives you access to the Windows 8 Advanced Boot Options, a set of commands that enable you to customize the way Windows 8 starts.

Windows 8 displays the Advanced Options screen.

Ⓐ Click System Restore to revert your system to an earlier configuration.

Ⓑ Click System Image Recovery to restore a system image backup.

Ⓒ Click Automatic Repair to repair startup problems.

Ⓓ Click Command Prompt to run a command-line program.

⑦ Click Startup Settings.

Windows 8 displays the Startup Settings screen.

⑧ Click Restart.

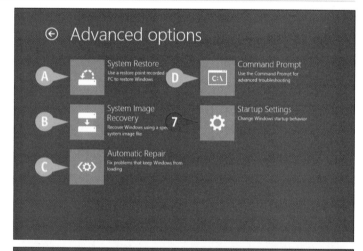

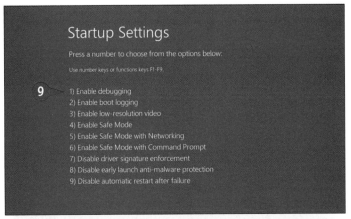

Windows 8 restarts your PC and then displays the Startup Settings screen.

9 Press the number of the command you want to run.

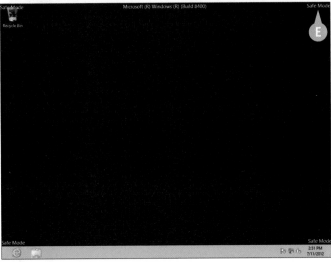

E If you start your computer in Safe Mode, Windows 8 displays 'Safe Mode' in each corner of the screen.

TIP

More Options!

Here is a summary of the Advanced Boot Options commands:

- **Enable Debugging:** Enables remote debugging of the Windows 8 kernel.
- **Enable Boot Logging:** Logs the boot process in a text file named ntbtlog.txt.
- **Enable Low-Resolution Video:** Loads with the display set to 640x480 and 256 colors.
- **Enable Safe Mode:** The three Safe Mode options enable you to run a barebones version of Windows 8 for troubleshooting.
- **Disable Driver Signature Enforcement:** Prevents Windows 8 from checking whether device drivers have digital signatures.
- **Disable Early Launch Anti-Malware Driver:** Prevents Windows 8 from scanning device drivers for malware during startup.
- **Disable Automatic Restart After Failure:** Prevents Windows 8 from restarting automatically when the system crashes.

Index

Index

Index

Power icon, 26
power on self test (POST), 140
Print Management, 9
program event, 134
program files, 267
programs
    compatibility mode, 150–151
    crashes, 156, 164, 268
    default programs, 82, 83
    elevated privileges, 148–149
    Paint graphics program, 82, 118
    pinning of, 4, 20–21
    sharing of, 248
    third-party ISO creation program, 95
    third-party programs, 106, 119, 121

Q

Quick Access Toolbar, 48–49

R

RAID (redundant array of inexpensive disks), 100
Read & Execute permission, 56
Read permission, 54, 56, 252–253
read receipt, 191, 234–235
read-only files, 90–91
Read/Write permission, 54
ReadyBoost technology, 152–153
recovery drive
    need for using, 156, 268
    resetting computer from, 270–273
    running Refresh Your PC from, 158–159
    USB recovery drive, 272–273, 275, 281
recovery environment (RE), 158, 270, 272, 280–283
recovery tools, 280–283
Recycle Bin, 267
red eye, 114–115
redundant array of inexpensive disks (RAID), 100
Refresh Your PC, 156–159, 270, 280–281
"remembering" information
    cookies, 216
    credentials, 243, 249
    folder windows, 92
    login information, 211
    passwords, 210
    settings, 172
Remote Desktop, 246–247
removable disk, 72, 105
Repair Your Computer, 159, 271, 275, 281
Reset Your PC, 268–271, 280–281
resiliency, 101
Resource Monitor, 9
restart shortcut, 13
restore points, 276–279
ribbon commands, 48–49
rich media environment, 110
Rich Text Document files, 82, 118
ripping, 126–127
rogue/runaway app, 154–155

S

Safe Mode, 278–279, 283
Safe Senders list, 226–227
SAS drive, 100
SATA drive, 100
screen resolution, 151
search engines, 146–147, 176–177
Search index, 146–147
search system, 36
secure desktop mode, 64–65
security, compromised, 66
Security screen, 67
sensitive files, 98
Service Set Identifier (SSID), 254
Services (administrative tool), 9
session cookies, 217
settings, synchronization of, 50–51
Sharing Wizard, 54–55, 250
shortcut icons, 14–15, 20
shortcut keys, 15, 138–139
shortcuts
    creating, 14
    keyboard, 138–139
    restart, 13–14
    shutdown, 15
shrink size, 107
shutdown tile, 12–15
signing in/signing on, 66–67, 71. See also logging on
SkyDrive app, 6
SmartScreen Filter, 233
SMTP (Simple Mail Transport Protocol), 204
Snap To feature, 142–143
sounds/sound scheme, 39, 134–135
spam, 204, 225–231
spell checker, 200
spoofing, 232
Sports app, 6
spyware, 62, 278
spyware protection, 62
SSID (Service Set Identifier), 254
standard port 25, 204
standard user account, 42, 44, 59, 148–149
Start menu, 18–19
Start screen, 2, 4–8, 14, 18, 162
starting computer, preventing others from, 72–73
starting Windows 8, unable to, 158
startup key (system key), 72–73
storage pool, creating, 100–101
storage space, 98, 100, 190, 198–199
Store app, 6–7
streaming, 130–131
Suggested Sites slice, 186
SuperFetch, 152
surfing, 162, 164, 178, 181, 186–187, 214–215
synchronization, 50–51
system checkpoint, 276
System Configuration, 8, 9
system files, refreshing, 156–159
system image backup, 274–275

Index

Read Less–Learn More®

There's a Visual book for every learning level...

Simplified®

The place to start if you're new to computers. Full color.

- Computers
- Creating Web Pages
- Digital Photography
- Internet
- Mac OS
- Office
- Windows

Teach Yourself VISUALLY™

Get beginning to intermediate-level training in a variety of topics. Full color.

- Access
- Computers
- Digital Photography
- Dreamweaver
- Excel
- Flash
- HTML
- iLife
- iPhoto
- Mac OS
- Office
- Photoshop
- Photoshop Elements
- PowerPoint
- Windows
- Wireless Networking
- Word
- iPad
- iPhone
- WordPress
- Muse

Top 100 Simplified® Tips & Tricks

Tips and techniques to take your skills beyond the basics. Full color.

- Digital Photography
- eBay
- Excel
- Google
- Internet
- Mac OS
- Office
- Photoshop
- Photoshop Elements
- PowerPoint
- Windows

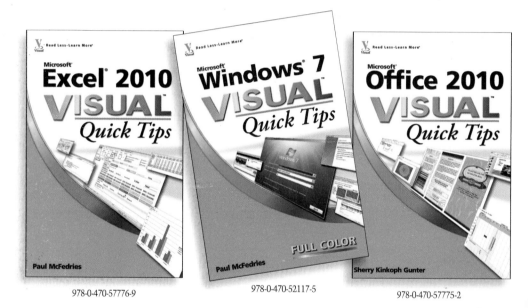